Pollmighty and Votepecker

A 'VERSE-A-STYLE' RAGA OF POLITICAL SAGA

UMAMAHESH SHISTA

Notion Press Media Pvt Ltd

No. 50, Chettiyar Agaram Main Road,
Vanagaram, Chennai, Tamil Nadu – 600 095

First Published by Notion Press 2021
Copyright © Umamahesh Shista 2021
All Rights Reserved.

ISBN 978-1-63886-515-5

Dedicated

To

All Creations of God

CONTENTS

ACKNOWLEDGEMENT

(Hearts That Matter)

I firstly wish to extend my soulful gratitude to my mother,

Late Mrs. Manikyam Sista, who always fostered a strong sense of spiritual as well as social discipline into the family, under the able guidance of my father, Late Mr. Hareeshwarasarma Sista.

As a Green Horn in the art of writing, I acknowledge the deep commitment and sincere efforts of Mrs. Bala Rao, my English teacher, in laying the first brick of a strong foundation in English language which helped me in carving and shaping my thoughts in the form of a book.

I am grateful to my relatives, friends, and well-wishers for being a constant source of inspiration and support.

My very special thanks to Brigadier Raghavendra Rao (Retd),

Major PT Choudary (Retd) and Mr. Franklin Noronha for introducing me to and guiding me through the publishing process in this maiden venture.

And finally, many thanks to the proofreader, book title and cover designer, and my ever-supportive, fantastic critic and a true companion through thick and thin of my life, my wife Mrs. Mandeep Shista.

PREFACE

It was in the year 2011 that I happened to meet my friend's Post-Graduate son, who was in search of a job that would further benefit him with global prospects in future. We discussed about various organizations that were engaged in hiring bright freshers, offered them good pay packages for some years and later sent them to different countries to expand their professional horizon.

As our conversation amplified from domestic preferences to global arena, I casually asked him, "You are young and dynamic. I have also observed that you are interested in national affairs. Why don't you consider Politics as a career option? I am sure you will certainly give your best to society, as an upcoming leader of the masses."

For the next few minutes, I witnessed the oscillating expressions on his face, failingly trying to display an attitude, unperturbed by my suggestion.

"No, Uncle! Politics is not my cup of tea. I am not good at decision making for the masses and public welfare on a mega scale. If I don't get success elsewhere, maybe I can consider your suggestion, but not at present." His ambiguity in finding a suitable career option for himself and his confidence in rejecting my suggestion without a second thought, opened a new chapter in my thought process on the magnitude of the term 'Politics'.

Dear Readers, the next ten years of my life provided me sufficient food for thought on this theme and here I am, presenting my first Mega Politico Venture, **POLLMIGHTY AND VOTEPECKER**, in the form of duologues, along with commentaries for clarity in the minds of the readers, providing multi- dimensional aspects to connect the dots with all institutions of society.

INTRODUCTION

POLLMIGHTY AND VOTEPECKER

Popular Politics, the Black Hole of vices, has endured infinite amount of criticism and hatred. A child that has been nurtured to become a punching bag for the guardians has not grown to dawn the mantle of the savior of the people. Christened in Greek to mean the **Affairs of the state**, it has seldom been understood and allowed to become a stately affair. It has assumed the form of an entity that is destructive and full of vices. Even the practitioners of the profession cry foul and accuse their opponents for **politicizing** serious issues.

A politician is expected to practice **Politics** as any other professional does. The unethical practices of the politicians need no mention as they are known even to the most apolitical citizen. The propriety and accountability of the unholy practices in politics have no takers and yet all parties take credit for serving the people. The infidelity of the politicians is considered inherent to the profession. Infidels are created by the system they are operating in to serve the system.

An individual leader or a group of leaders who pledge to serve the people represent them not only politically but also in all aspects of social life. Whereas, in an imperial form of governance, the subjects are a reflection of their ruler, in a democratic set up the rulers are chosen by the subjects and hence are representatives of the people, projecting and propagating all their vices and virtues to the outside world. The pride and the pathos of the common citizens all over the world are measured by the leadership that the nations showcase. Sounder the voice of the common citizen, stronger the leadership.

However, in a world reverberating with the noise of power and the echoes of wealth, the inner voice of the common citizen finds no way out. The weight of high stakes involved in the struggle for survival by holding on to the position of power stifles the inner voice of the leader as much as it chokes the voice of the follower.

Endless vows of the common people and the helplessness of the leader to alleviate them have equally compelling reasons. Whereas, the follower can take the liberty of blaming the leader for the evils of the society, the leader cannot counter-attack because the power and the position of the leader is sustained by the very follower.

The follower can vengefully exercise the freedom to prosecute the leader for betrayal by denying the vote. The leader has no such options and has to praise the follower, for it is the follower who brings the leader to power. The dynamics of the political game do not facilitate a free, transparent and a heart to heart duologue between the two.

The interplay of various components of the society which are the author's reflections on a disintegrating and degenerating political world order are presented in the form of a duologue between the leader and the follower.

The eternal drama of politics has been described in 700 verses under 70 chapters. The verses cover a gamut of issues relating to politics, society, and the daily living. They display the essence of governance in principle and its distorted form in practice, taking the reader on a journey to the corridors of power through the meandering lanes of greed, ambition, bribery, and sycophancy.

The writing gives an insight into the nuances of politics, its perils, privileges, and pageantry. **The verses do not target any individual, gender, group, race, religion, or country.** They highlight the need to understand and practice individual morality to attain collective prosperity. They also exhort the reader to propagate social and financial honesty for the progress and wellbeing of every individual.

Citizenship by birth ensures inheritance of assets of the country to be shared by all and stamps every individual with an identity that gives a sense of security in numbers. Every citizen of the world is provided with such facilities with an expectation that the individual contributes positively to sustain and improve them for the posterity.

The structure of society demands that every individual earns a livelihood for self and the family and in this process contributes to the society for the services provided. The mode of earning dictates the health of the society. Exchange of money is an inevitable process. Unlike natural processes wherein matter flows only in one direction, that is, from higher level to lower level, exchange of money is a two-way process. More often it takes the unnatural path, that is, from lower level to higher level. Hence the term **'Siphoning of Money'**.

A career carved with the chisel of hard work and the hammer of honesty amounts to a healthy and just contribution.

Unfortunately, personal ambition and unwillingness of the industrious lot to contribute for the undeserving and dead weights of the society makes an honest mind susceptible to corruption.

Forced corruption brought about by the individual or the society leaves escape routes for the wrong doers. Dishonesty, gross or subtle, financial or moral, becomes legal or illegal depending on the degree and proportion. No society is immune to corruption, only the tolerance levels differ.

The verses showcase *the web of money and might, every mighty spoke of the web being the leader and the delicate yarn—the follower. The leader and the follower together make the fabric that is woven around the hub of essential elements in life.*

The interaction and the bonding of the two culminates into an organized activity of politics with the portfolios of the leader and the follower. The journey up or down the political ladder shows one's success or failure; crowded the ladder, murkier the struggle to reach the top. The journey down feels bumpier than the ascent.

The duologue in the book is between the leader who begins the political journey as a Vote Pecker and attains the status of an Almighty Being after being brought into power, and the follower who begins the election process as a Poll Mighty and eventually attains the status of a Lesser Being after being bought for power.

The leader portrays self as the servant of the masses and pecks for every vote. After the elections, the victorious leader has all the powers of governance. The leader obliges the voter by meeting the just and unjust demands placed by the latter.

However, no leader ever intimidates every individual follower, by word or by sword, to follow corrupt practices. Followers have absolute authority to exercise their will to practice honesty at their level. There are inspiring examples of people displaying supreme moral and financial honesty, though working in a completely corrupt environment. Their clan would grow if citizens stop fleecing one another and thus put an end to the chain reaction of bribery at individual level.

The verses speak out the mind of the leader who lacks courage, to castigate the voter for being responsible for corrupting, and exploiting the fellow commoner. Ironically, the leader is solely blamed for spreading corruption in the society and it is the leader who must go back to the corrupt voter with a promise to uproot corruption.

The voice of the **Almighty Being** is the voice of every person voted to power by people. People practice dishonesty at micro level and expect honesty at macro level.

No leader dares to blame the follower for spreading corruption for fear of falling out of favour and eventually losing power.

The compulsions of politics are brought forth in a conversation between the **Poll Mighty Voter**, hereinafter called '**Devotee**' and the **Vote Pecker Leader**, hereinafter called '**Devoted**.**

As the book begins, stage is set in the midst of a political battle, wherein the **Devotee**, who is unwilling to participate in the battle—the Election Process—is being engaged by the **Devoted** in an enlightening Political Discourse.

CHAPTER 1

THE DEVOTEE'S DILEMMA

Said the Devotee:

"Having witnessed the verbal and physical battles

My serene, still mind shakes and rattles;

How can the ones that spew venom

Bring life to me, my daughter, my son;

This tussle for votes gets ever murkier

No more will I bear the pain, Dear Savior;

Whither people's rule, whither democracy

Lording over all, the dance of demons crazy;

Freedom to preach evil, body soul blemished

Deeds to shame the devil, a hundred Satans unleashed;

The Devotee said:

I observe the quarrels and abuses thrown by the contesting parties at one another during the elections and get disillusioned and scared as it disturbs my peace of mind.

When the parties with their candidates contesting elections have such strong differences and animosity, how can they serve the subjects in a just manner!

In the battle for votes, the mudslinging and swearing between the parties gets ever vicious and unbearable.

Is this what is people's rule and democracy where the powerful behave like demons and display their unchallenged sovereignty?

The preachers of democracy are corrupt in body and soul and thus behave in a manner that would put the devil to shame.

Spreading forest fires, roots and shoots corrupting

Scorching leaves and flowers, with fruits of sin erupting;

Skies in anguish rant, echoes of misfortune heard

Unmoved they pursue power, immoral deed, and word;

Hapless one I see, crime and passion gory

Watching march sinister, sounding tunes of glory;

Not one seems sincere, that begs for every vote

I shall deny mine and thank my soul's revolt;

Crime, injustice, corruption would you see, O Leader!

Or defend your clan in battle, fighting as loyal pleader?"

The flames of corruption engulf the society, burning through the various sections of the society. Such a society would always beget harmful results.

The deeds of the rulers predict pain and misery but the rulers heed not to the warning and continue with their base acts.

I am a helpless witness and victim of the passion and ambition of the rulers who commit crime and yet praise themselves.

None of these rulers work with commitment that they promise while begging for votes. I wish to refrain from voting as a mark of revolt.

Would you, the esteemed leader, appreciate your role in the midst of crime and corruption perpetrated by your ruling clan or turn a blind eye to defend them?

CHAPTER 2
PURPOSE OF PREACHING

Hearing the plight of the Devotee, the divine face did smile
Truth the Devoted held, the Devotee blew it a mile;

Day of reckoning dawned, for unsaid truth's hearing
For tortured soul's redemption, for bonded mind's flowering;

Said the Devoted to Devotee, "Lose not heart on illusions
In distress you need call me, draw no wrong conclusions;

Maze of life deludes, morons, naïve, erudite
Know your role in battle, before giving up a fight;

Statesmanship for all, though perilous and demanding
State of calm you beget, with will for understanding;

The anguish of the devotee made the devoted smile as the devoted held the truth and the devotee got estranged from it.

Time had come for the concealed truth to be revealed to the tortured devotee and set the mind free of all misgivings and doubts.

Said the Devoted assuring the Devotee, "Do not panic and come to wrong conclusions but repose faith in me when in trouble.

Life, being full of uncertainties and mysteries, puzzles the wise as well as the ignorant. The battle of life is to be fought with a clear understanding of one's role.

Politics and governance are fraught with danger and difficulties. One can handle them with quietude, provided one is willing to understand its nuances.

Lamentations as yours, millions share no wonder

Meek witness to the game, of reckless loot and plunder;

Share you may not, but all, sans you, not absolved

Nectar of corruption found, in many a cup dissolved;

Heed not to cries, that bemoan the death of honesty

Fruits of greed they eat, that poison the soul, though tasty;

Hear from me for once, the truth of self revealed

Chest of wisdom spilling, thought nor word concealed;

Here I sound the death knell, for one's vice and exploitation

Summons to the tortured devotee, that roams in expectation."

Millions of subjects harbour the same feelings as yours but are quiet spectators to the unjust deeds of the corrupt people.

A few like you may not be a party to the shady deals but the majority are partaking of the sweet returns of corruption.

All cry hoarse over the thinning down of honesty but are engaged in dishonest acts. The profit may be alluring, but in the end, it weakens the soul.

I beacon you to listen to the words of wisdom which would reveal the truth that I will disclose without hiding the facts or holding anything back.

I would forever banish the doubts about the sources of crime and injustice prevailing in the society and not allow them to torment your mind anymore."

CHAPTER 3

DUTY TOWARDS THE COUNTRY

Said the Devoted:

"Guided by instinct, evolves marvel of nature—Life
Defending the clan fiercely, with claws, fangs, or knife;

The mighty rule the forest, weaklings just one tree
The beast stands its ground, humans their dear country;

Guarding bushes, swamps and skies, survives humanism
Living for self and own kind, spirit of nationalism;

Grouping for one cause, sharing filth or beauty
Thrives human society, with vested social duty;

Swarm of bees, school of fish or healthy herds bovine
Toil together to fend evil, and enjoy life divine;

Said the Devoted to the Devotee:

The nature's miracle, that is life, works and progresses on instincts. All creatures preserve themselves using the weapons that nature has given them.

The powerful animals rule the forest and the smaller ones survive on a tree. The animals defend their territory just as human beings protect their country.

The human society thrives on land, in water and in the air to propagate its own species and comes together as a nation for collective safety and security.

Humans unite to share the wealth and the poverty. The social set up demands that they shoulder the responsibilities for the common good.

All social creatures that live in groups and herds tend to their duties and prosper as a unit.

Need they gain synergy, hearing lofty sermons
Born with a sense of duty, social than we humans;

Gifted are we folks, pampering our sensations
Nestling in security, and warmth of Mother Nation;

Blood and sweat as worship, we repay what we shared
Honour, Pride, Elan, for one and all, none spared;

Wisdom gained wisdom shared, worthy of veneration
Baton held for seeking arms, gift for new generation;

Shun beggars, pious or tattered, the dead weight of society
Sick minds in healthy bodies, a burden heed nor pity."

The animals follow the social diktats instinctively and display a stronger social bonding than the humans.

Citizens of all the nations of the world enjoy the freedom and luxury provided by the social set up. They are blessed and are pampered by the society they created.

Nation demands that the subjects work hard in return of the obligation, pride and identity bestowed on them.

The wisdom and knowledge gained over centuries is respected and preserved when passed on to the new generation which should be equally willing to accept the gift of knowledge.

Those able bodies who care not for the social duties and survive on another's labour need to be left uncared, notwithstanding their garb as they are parasites with a sick mind trapped in a healthy body.

CHAPTER 4

WAYS OF EARNING LIVELIHOOD

"Now know the fields of harvest," thus learned leader spake

"Made sanguine battlefields, with honest lives at stake;

Earning for dear life, prodded by one's nature

Human form reacts, morphed as every creature;

Sincere service for some, simple heart's delight

Mind at peace with oneself, augurs none to fight;

Hoards wealth aplenty, acts thus shady, sleazy

Sweat no guarantee for fortunes, cries the sloth and lazy;

Service, barter, begging, thriving on charity

Means to earn a morsel, needs action with clarity;

The Devoted said: I shall tell you about the different means of livelihood that we employ to achieve peace. But, in the process, we turn the struggle into a battle.

All creatures make efforts to keep body and soul together, but it is the human being that takes any form to deceive or cheat in order to make profits.

A small minority takes pride in being honest and is content with what they get with sincere, hard work. Peaceful co-existence is their way of life.

There exists a section of the society that accumulates wealth by employing dubious means. They believe that sincerity and hard work does not pay enough.

Whatever the means to achieve the end, business, begging or barter, all call for clarity of thought if one has to live with dignity.

Fear, guilt, benediction, drives one to be generous

Sins erupting as never, to lend a hand are numerous;

That thrives on will without, humble meekly beggar

One that thaws will within, scary rustic mugger;

Threatens one with misfortune, souls timid and guilty

Injures one body frail, with violence and cruelty;

Wants drives the pious, to pursue work dignified

Greed nails honesty, on altar—thus crucified;

Begets one so simple, scanty meager exploits

Many-fold one makes, that naive ones exploits."

People indulge in charitable works for fear of god, due to a guilty feeling of being selfish or for having a generous nature. However, sinful acts go on unabated.

Those who earn a living by begging subtly shake the conscience of their host. The crude robbers rob their victim by intimidation.

The beggar threatens the sinful and guilty host with misfortune if not served. The rustic robber demands by using violent means.

People work with honesty and earn their living and satisfy their wants. When the wants take the form of greed, they sacrifice their honesty.

The ones that lead a simple life with piety make lesser fortunes compared to those who cheat others for their benefit. Profits multiply many folds when one exploits others.

CHAPTER 5

EXCHANGE OF MONEY AND POWER

"Business, service, theft, charity, makes life's dwelling

Limbs of ambition flailing, cause of egos swelling;

Alluring but daunting, are the ways of business

Service, theft, charity warp it in viscous cess;

Held in place with service, a measure of strength within

Meanest actions tall and stout, honest service thin;

Scalp of business tormented, crown of thorns at work

Fraught with blemish aplenty, shadows of misfortune lurk;

Easy road the server treads, losses kept at bay

Deeds sincere or crafty, more or less but pay;

People resort to different means of livelihood. Business, job, charity, theft and begging are the ways of sustenance. Ambition to rise higher and an urge to earn more makes a person intolerant and indifferent to others.

Business has high returns and is attractive but is equally challenging and risky. Trading incorporates all other means to make profits.

Business calls for sincere service to earn profit and gain strength and reputation. However, for huge and quick gains one resorts to dishonest means. Majority of traders fall prey to greed and an urge to progress fast by all means possible.

A trader has to constantly apply new ideas and plan new strategies to compete and stay in business. A small mistake or careless planning can ruin the business.

Those who prefer to render services are safer as they incur no losses. They may not be sincere in their work but are paid.

Thread of charity runs smooth, without kinks or knots
Free flow of fortune, from Haves to Have-nots;

Wall of theft built alone, with bricks of desires tall
Raised with greedy ambition, forcing rise and fall;

Humans big or small, trapped in healthy body
Fair or dark the skin, with forms cute or gaudy;

Wish Brain of business ticking, heart of service beating
Blood of charity pure, limbs of labour sweating;

Need clean breath of ethics, cleansing blood impure
Sign of healthy nation, prize of Peace for sure."

Some indulge in charitable work and form a medium to serve the needy. Services to the socially weaker sections is welcome and finds many takers.

Many lazy ones have desire to get rich without labouring for it. They resort to stealing and amass wealth. Stronger the desire bigger the theft.

All the citizens of a nation, rich or poor, fair or dark, strong or weak, beautiful or ugly, wish for wellbeing and prosperity.

All demand honesty in dealings, a sincere service, and a fair way of distribution of wealth to the needy and deserving. Fair flow of wealth would empower the weak.

Ethical conduct in all fields of life would remove injustice and corruption. This would make the nation strong and ensure lasting peace to one and all.

CHAPTER 6
CAREER SOCIALLY PATRONIZED

Asked the Devotee:

"When will world watch, wards wishing and not wince

Carve a career in politics, no words pray do mince;

None heard to brave the odds, and invite for self-disgrace

Statesmen clan of yours, young hearts whence embrace;

Curse and insults heaped on job, for souls venerable

Cradle of crime—governance, waiting for child ignoble;

Parents chaste or born of sin, pray their child has power

Bowl of politics not their choice, welcome misery's shower;

Reveal to me the truth you see, Mighty King Devoted

Sinful are your words and deeds, why then are you voted?"

The Devotee asked the Devoted:

Without parrying my question please tell me when students will opt for a career in politics.

No student would dare to take up a career in politics and invite ridicule. None would associate oneself with your tribe.

The respectable citizens detest a job that is abused and cursed. Politics is considered to be full of crime and criminals and is fit for people of ill repute.

All parents whether pious or otherwise wish that their wards occupy seat of power but are not ready to make them politicians.

If politics and the politicians are looked down upon and hated, then why do people vote them and give them power to rule?

Said the Devoted:

"Children born of and in politics, Devoted or the Devotee
You set a thief to catch a thief, and they steal a share of booty;

Harbour no doubts child's play, is education of my tricks
Survival dear Devotee, no child's play but unholy politics;

Teacher of no will for civics, taught us quite a lesson
The pupil warped the juvenile thought, saw the need lessen;

Physical laws easy to tame, tighten a few nut-bolts
Human laws snap at will, mind, not machine revolts;

Few need to taste the king's nectar, sapless political science
Subjects take the subjects, that ensure a cheque one signs."

The Devoted answered thus:

You elect the leader hoping that your leader will punish the wrong doers. Instead, the leader, whether a ward of a ruler or a common citizen, joins the robbers.

Teaching the tricks of politics is not a difficult task. One can learn it watching others. Once one joins politics one realizes how difficult it is to survive without resorting to corruption.

Children are taught Civics and the process of governance by the teachers who themselves have no interest and are biased against it. The child when not taught with zeal loses interest and finds it worthless.

The student finds it easy to understand the scientific laws that do not change with time. It is easy to manage a machine as it does not revolt but human beings amend or break laws to suit their convenience. Hence difficult to control.

The science of politics not being interesting for learning, finds less takers. Students prefer education that ensures good financial returns.

CHAPTER 7

CAREER SOCIALLY ORPHANED

"Gifted some find security, in inherited profession

New tasks new challenges, is another's aspiration;

Promising rewards fulfilling, goal of every will

A few values none, but a potion of thrill;

Amassing wealth aplenty, greedy folks' intent

Noble some sweat, for bleeding heart's content;

Mind—measure of wealth, a bowl full of greed

Turns heart to stone, that knows not to bleed;

Contentment a sedative, keeps the crafty at bay

Hampers march of progress, gobblers of glory say;

Some wards are lucky to be initiated into a profession set up by their parents and are content with pursuing the established business. Some are adventurous and are driven by an urge to explore new avenues.

All desire a satisfying and monetarily lucrative occupation. There are a few who prefer a life and job full of thrill and adventure.

Some work untiringly to earn plenty of wealth. Their hunger for wealth has no limit. A few good Samaritans take pains to serve the underprivileged.

A simple and honest mind is the true wealth of a person. Greed and ambition make one indifferent to pain and sorrow of others.

Those who wish to amass wealth find contentment to be a hindrance in their progress. They do not find satisfaction in leading an unknown commoner's life.

Excess of contentment, a bliss in brimless measure

Excess of wealth an addiction, sans humane pleasure;

Glory heaped upon, and wealth unfathomably showered

Magic wand of politics, Heaven upon Earth lowered;

Dream of one and all, game of man and mammon

Treacherous path for elite, less trodden by common;

Governance, game of life, acted fair or foul

Sunshine turns one swan, nightfall turns one owl;

Politics, crime, criminals, play in every relation

Honesty, trust, brotherhood, all if met cremation."

One who is satisfied with whatever one gets by hard and sincere work is always in a blissful state. One who hankers for more wealth and fame lives in perpetual anxiety.

In the profession of politics, the leader is gifted with name, fame, and wealth by the followers. Politics has the power to make available the luxuries of the heaven.

All human beings desire to enjoy the privileges of the politicians but find the path fraught with danger. Only the powerful or wealthy people choose this profession.

Life at all levels demands good governance. The ones that govern people's affairs use fair and unfair means and thus become famous or infamous.

Human activities are based on relations with one another. Honesty and trust nurture a healthy relation. Crime and ill-will thrive in the absence of trust and a feeling of brotherhood.

CHAPTER 8

THE DESIRE FOR A LEADER

"Leaders," said the Devotee, "is the rightful wish of the led
Society bereft of them I fear, would leave the nations dead;

For clearing hurdles countless, lighting path for commons
Need I choose—a common man, for guide even demons."

Said Devoted, "Dear one, none is left with option
Leaders drive desire's cart, run on wheels of compulsion;

I for one would vouch for you, being gifted with that throne
Some stubborn struggle hard, though pelted, canted, thrown;

Why you need a beacon, ever pondered yourself
Flare path never a wish, a light who is to oneself;

Human society needs noble beings as leaders to guide them. Tribes, society or nations cannot be governed without able leaders.

The people need someone to lead them through difficulties, but they depend on those who eventually lead them to disaster.

The Devoted said:

We wish for good leaders but soon run out of options because power corrupts them. The leaders also have no choice but to be corrupt to stay in power.

I occupy the seat of power and surely know that there are some leaders who strive to serve you even if they face stiff opposition.

If one does not have the wisdom to guide one's own destiny, one falls prey to the many leaders one creates, hoping to be tutored and led safely.

Rejoice Dear Devotee, making hay in meadows

Leave me scorching in sun, for you, I cast shadows;

Incisions of insults deep, heaps of hatred I counter

Serve you not as you desire, poor me in for banter;

Wish if yours exacting, should one dare deny

Trust you stuffed sublimates, should I ever annoy;

Serve you with devotion, lest I fall from grace

Falter I and my might, vanishes without a trace;

Rake Grey matter a while, to hit chords harmonic

Nay play tunes of discord, divine or demonic."

Most of the people want a leader to solve their problems so that they can enjoy without facing hardship, leaving the leader to toil and struggle for them.

I, the leader, enjoy your favour till I meet your just or unjust demands. When I fail to oblige, I am held responsible for all the evils of the society.

Even when your unjust demands are not fulfilled, I am to lose the trust you placed in me to do good to the people.

I am expected to serve the people with devotion and honesty but if I don't favour the corrupt people then they would strip me of my powers.

People need to think before placing unfair demands and let the leaders discharge their duties for which the people chose them.

THE INDIVIDUAL AND THE SOCIETY

Said the Devoted:

"Behold, Dear Devotee in splendor this collage
If patch and plaster society, a perfect form—mirage;

Paints each one, that has a brush with society
A colour smacked on it, held in one's propriety;

Varied shades chromatic, splashed on canvas
Many colours changed, by each one to canvass;

Picture thus painted, a reflection of feelings nurtured
Portrait distorted by people, society thus fractured;

I the revered one, idol of mass desires
One among the equals, to lead one aspires;

Said the Devoted to Devotee:

Watch the society in different shapes and shades. It looks patchy and fragmented and that is its true form. A perfectly carved society does not exist.

Each citizen has to interact with others and contribute in building and shaping the society. People's involvement and contribution makes the society weak or strong.

People of varied interests and intentions add variety to the social fabric. Many change their views and principles to suit their ambitions, adding more variety.

The structure of the society shows the intent, dreams, and ambitions of the people. A fragmented or a healthy society reflects the thoughts of the people.

I, the leader, symbolize the aspirations and hope of the people. I am a common citizen, but I am idolized as I lead the people.

Hope mundane, genre sores on classic wings

Dreams of lowly subjects, nightmares see we kings;

I, a commoner once, steer a course divergent

From my trusted makers, casting votes cogent;

Lives one among the many, of that an idol cast

To dispel doubts and shake faith, born an iconoclast;

Pray some of you, but lives with you and lead

Your intent nor your wishes, fuel pyre of greed;

Wish honest ones for social cleansing, desire a crown

Share not the load of discontent, that fear to drown."

People have expectations, great or little, from the leader which they hope to get fulfilled to their liking. We the leaders find it difficult to please all.

I am the leader who was once a commoner and hence know their plight. They have voted me to power but I as a leader have a different view about governance.

You choose a leader from amongst yourselves and expect the leader to be honest and serve the people. But I am a leader born to differ and clear your misconceptions.

You want your leader to be with you and lead you to progress. However, your wish for personal gains and favours does not allow you to kill your greed for the benefit of the society.

The one who desires to lead should be ready for social cleansing, even against the will of the outlaws. Those who are afraid of losing their fortune would not share social responsibility.

CHAPTER 10

MONEY, MIGHT AND MORALS

Shows the wise one, the social web in making

Devotee's doubts set, the devoted brain raking;

Said the Devoted:

"Dear Devotee not, let me rest on my laurels

Society—a web of money, might and morals;

Will to survive adds substance, for shaky web to hold

A life of comfort sans toil, invites miseries untold;

Bearing the weight in center, the hub of morality

Symbol of strength, and seat of social identity;

Bound to the hub—money, the almighty spoke

Ever glorified by all, ill of wealth none spoke;

The Devotee requested the Devoted to describe the social setup that governs the lives of the people. The Devoted summoning wisdom thus replied to the Devotee;

The Devoted said:

The society, being formed of power, wealth and services that we define, constantly expects something from us.

Struggle for survival keeps the society going. Majority of them suffer because they want to earn a living without hard and sincere work.

The honest people add strength to the society and prevent its collapse. These few honest ones are the true identity of the society at large.

Money makes the all-powerful spoke of the web, that holds the structure together. Though it is the cause of all the miseries, no one talks ill of wealth.

Yarn of labour spun, around the spoke of wealth

Thus forms the web, the measure of social health;

Strong winds of adversity, leaves the web shaken

Trinity that forms the web, reason for fabric broken;

Shower of gentle rain, irrigates the social farm

Seeds are sure to shoot, Sun if friendly warm;

Heavens open in downpour, bring wrath in deluge

Sun and rain in excess, heap up destruction huge;

Wealth of mindless plunder, scorch and sweep its call

Dam of wisdom crumbles, high and mighty fall."

Hard work put in by the subjects along with Money contributed by them and by the state build a healthy social structure.

Circumstances test the strength of the society. The strength of the three elements makes or breaks the society.

When all the factors that govern the progress of a society are in reasonable measure, the society thrives.

Excess of any factor disturbs the balance and the society crumbles just as excess of sunshine scorches the Earth and torrential rain sweeps all that comes in its way.

When a section of society amasses wealth by unfair means, the same wealth corrupts the mind, destroying reason and bringing down even the wise and powerful.

CHAPTER 11
THE VOLUNTARY SINNER

Said the Devoted:

"What becomes of you Dear Devotee, decides your ability

Fellow commoner to compete, a test of stability;

Will to labour sincerely, a trait found so rare

Vile is the mighty mind, that learnt not to share;

Few amongst you, soften skills to stretch

And set fair means, for success to fetch;

Fear all but few, to sail and steer in storm

Ambition rock hard, without soul or form;

One so crafty calls, honesty nay to invest

Millions of such brood, clone self to infest;

The Devoted said:

The abilities of a person are responsible for earning a living in a world that progresses and evolves better when fellow beings test their skills to perform better.

A thin minority finds hard work rewarding enough to be pursued as a guiding principle. The successful and the powerful are reluctant to share their fortunes that were earned with unfair means.

A very few ones like you cultivate clean habits and dealings and hope to get rewarded for your sincerity.

Most choose to follow a path of least resistance and are afraid of taking risks. Their ambitions are strong but lack spirit or commitment.

A cunning mind finds honesty a hurdle in its progress. A large majority of such people influence others to follow them.

Rivals for ever, are the haves and the have-nots
You hoard so you grow, other not and so rots;

A few mouths to feed, a few ills to attend
Nature's gift aplenty, Heavens to Earth descend;

Growing by the millions, species success story
In battle for survival, meeting end in glory;

Beast in animals springs up, nature fair dictates
Human fury unleashed, angel within hesitates;

Sin some not compelled, but do evil on volition
Greet enemy within, to form dreaded coalition."

The tussle between those who possess wealth and those who are deprived is eternal. One that amasses wealth prospers and the deprived one weakens further.

Lesser the population, lesser the demands, problems, and evils in the society. Nature grants all boons that humans wish to make this planet a heaven.

The human society thrives and prospers with ever increasing population, a testimony to its success. In this march to glory many a weakling perish.

Mother Nature sets rules to ensure the fittest creatures survive. In human society the greedy show no mercy and the noble ones choose not to fight.

Some people commit crime without any external compulsion. Their enemy lies within whom they befriend and stay away from virtue.

CHAPTER 12

THE GULLIBLE SINNER

Asks the Devotee:

"Why among the greedy brood, some not lured

What potion ensures illness—tamed or cured?"

Said the Devoted:

"Untouched by this evil, exists a blessed clan

Wading through the swamp, sporting feathers of swan;

Simple one may enjoy, awhile bliss of ignorance

Blissful walk of naïve, vice but overruns;

Devil of corruption hidden, not tamed if ignored

Deception kept awake, careless ones snored;

Like hunger, thirst, and sleep, should evil confront

Sulking ones stand down, chivalrous ones upfront;

The Devotee asked:

Why, not all are lured by the glitter of wealth. Do they have an antidote or immunity against corruption?

The Devoted replied that very few are unaffected by the filth around them. They wade through it as a swan wades through water without getting wet.

The simple ones enjoy the bliss of being ignorant of the lurking danger but soon confront the vice and the vicious ones.

Ignorance of the ways of the corrupt does not ensure safety of the gullible. One may pretend to be unaware and deceive self to sleep peacefully.

When people experience the force of this evil like other natural urges, the weak ones succumb to the pressure and the strong ones revolt against it.

Weak of mind that survive, line up on the knees
Cold wave of corruption, sees them shiver and freeze;

Spreads this Dear Devotee, epidemic of submission
Millions thus survive, in praise of unholy mission;

Does one care to know, ways of corrupt governance
Pyre of moral values, fire and fuel indifference;

Know for once, the form of system you dread
Brace up mind and soul, to prevent its spread;

Shun the daily grind, to make you worth your salt
Choke fuel and corrupt mill, brought to grinding halt.

The ones that cannot stand the forces of evil and succumb to them find themselves exploited by the corrupt.

This submissive state spreads throughout the masses and then they sing praises of the evil for their survival.

No one cares to understand the working of the corrupt people and that indifference results in the death of their moral values.

Once you understand the working of this corrupt system, you can at least prepare to stop it from spreading.

If you refrain from corrupt activities in earning your bread, you can starve the corrupt system and halt its march.

CHAPTER 13

THE ELITE SINNER

Said the Devoted:

"None is born elite, the elite though give birth

By millions spring the able, Alas! still the dearth;

Fortune winks at few, most with misfortune fought

The gifted begets one, the gift's produce a naught;

Noble strings of value, tug at virtue's cradle

Tames the horses, in leash in sturdy saddle;

Born to elite a boon, wealth aplenty for flaunting

Live up to carry the baton, task no doubt daunting;

Heir of elite step out, on call all assistance

To pave a way to glory, on path of least resistance;

The Devoted said:

One may be born to the elite parents but is not elite by birth. There are a large number of able-bodied people but a very few who deliver.

Some are born lucky, but a majority are less fortunate and have to struggle. The talented make a fortune but contribute nothing to the society.

Those who are born gifted are attached to noble values and are strong enough to maintain a dignified and pious lifestyle.

Blessed with wealth and virtues, the ward of the elite is vested with responsibilities to come up to the expectations of the parents.

The children of fortune have all the resources to face the world and succeed. For them life poses less problems and the journey to fame is easy.

Elitism the elixir, not gifted away by gods

Earned by labour loyal, courage to face all odds;

Child in the womb of talent, glory's lap its goal

Laps up fame and fortune, needs no corrupted soul;

One so adept labours less, pride of the nation

Noble soul's unrest, for rest to draw inspiration;

Lesser mortals labour, till destiny inborn defied

Park in seat of fame, means and ends unjustified;

Thorns or roses lay in bed, but weary sleeper dreams

To be or not to be the elite, the morbid society's cream."

Achievements and success are not bestowed as gifts but are earned with hard work and taking risk.

Those born to successful parents also seek success like their parents and being privileged can do so without staining their character.

One so privileged need not struggle like others and can get recognition by being upright and thus can be an inspiration to others.

The ones that are less fortunate struggle to overcome odds and win a privileged position. They have to resort to means fair and foul which are not morally justified.

Those chasing success know that their journey to fame will be full of problems, yet they wish to be the elite among the mediocre ones in the society.

CHAPTER 14
THE FORCED SINNER

Said the Devoted:

"Hear from me devotee, of minds born in sin

Born of corrupt souls, raised in palace or din;

No one born a sinner, none of soul satanic

Bred with bread and broth, earned with acts manic;

Every breath polluted, morsel laced with venom

Unfair means a duty, sadist service serum;

Mind tethered to vice, body led on harm's way

Journey down the childhood lane, malice held sway;

O! Devotee, child of sin, that thrives on evil consumption

Cursed one when comes of age, begs not for redemption;

The Devoted said:

Now I will tell you about the wards born to criminals. They may be born to rich parents in a palace or to poor in a hut.

One may be born to a sinner, but none is a born sinner. Being born to criminals one has to share the spoils earned by conceit.

Such an unlucky one grows in an unhealthy environment and is duty bound to follow the footsteps of the parents.

Since childhood one is influenced by the unholy practices and is inclined to harm others for personal gains.

A child who is thus brought up on evil means does not feel apologetic. Corruption is a way of life and such a one does not ask for salvation.

The blessed pleasure's child, in excess gets pampered

Locked its will in fortune's chest, all but will tampered;

One that tasted the bitter pill, as infant played in squalor

Twists and turns on bed of thorns, sleep a mark of valour;

Will for change wells up in chest, to set free in time adverse

In wealth or filth, if discontent, heeds not for good or worse;

Pressure within a feeble cry, born of self-revulsion

Scuffled by own hands, hapless soul's compulsion;

Blame it on frail bond, the human burden **Relation**

Deprive ward of honour, or honour social obligation."

A child given to luxury and unbridled pleasure is lost in the world of plenty and thus loses the will to question the parents and their deeds.

Those unfortunate ones born to poor lead a traumatic life and are deprived of basic needs. They find life a perpetual struggle for existence with no succor.

In difficult times one is propelled to force a change. The unhappy one, whether rich or poor, does not bother about the consequences to force a change.

Such one sometimes tries to impose will and break free to lead a pious life. Such acts of the young are promptly quashed.

Human relations are so exacting that the wayward ward honours the unjust demands of the relatives forgetting the duty towards the society.

CHAPTER 15

THE PATRONS OF MALICE

Hearing the interplay of individual and society

Devotee thus engaged the Devoted with piety:

Said the Devotee:

"Which entities sow, the seeds of social sin

To reap the harvest, the social borers within?"

Said the Devoted:

"The trinity of Giver, Seeker, and the Pleader

Three demigods, turning the greed's breeder;

With greed for higher gains, the Giver lays the bait

Instinct or compulsion, sets the Seeker's trait;

Earn or spurn the bait, choice of the Seeker

Victim or a victor, conscience is their maker;

The Devotee, having heard about the interaction between the sinners and the society, thus conversed with the Devoted:

Said the Devotee:

I wish to know about those who perpetuate sin and gain from creating sinners in the society that they live in.

Said the Devoted:

The three entities, the one who approves, the one who applies and the one who scrutinizes, when caught in the net of greed, become, and thus create the sinners.

A greedy Giver sets a trap for the greedy Seeker who willingly gets trapped for higher gains. Struggle for survival in a greedy society makes for a willing prey.

A duel of Conscience against the temptations decides whether one overcomes the greed and inspires society or succumbs to it and blames the society.

Pretend the holy pleader, to grope in the dark
Mouthful of morsel, watch-dogs forget to bark;

In the march for success, they fall from grace
A mad rush for fortunes, none pray lose the race;

Left in the lurch, are the gifted and deserving
Trot on crutches moral, lords thus left serving;

The battle turns uneven, trinity hand in glove
Meanest vie with morals, like vulture versus dove;

Trait of social malice, malice of social traitors
Predation of trinity, the trinity of predators."

One suggests many ways to change the society but finds no way or reason to change self. When one's wants are met one falls silent.

Everyone desires to be successful and make a fortune for themselves and the family. One tries all means fair or foul to win the race of survival.

A few honest ones find it difficult to cope up with the demands of the society and are thus left behind to serve the unworthy winners.

When the trinity subvert a fair game then the deserving ones do not get their dues. The struggle for success becomes biased and easier for the undeserving to win.

The corruption in the society is the contribution of every individual. Sometimes one feels cheated and at other one cheats others.

CHAPTER 16

THE BRIBING GAME

Said the Devoted:

"Where do you find devotee, bloated with self esteem

Did mirror reflect a predator, or painted you a victim?

Unmindful of deeds, you hanker for a few alms

Slip ahead of the honest, if need be greasing palms;

Your face one so placid, at will took different forms

Deceived you thought others, but self-deception harms;

Tried capturing happiness, wished deserts landscaped

Wind of justice blew sand dunes, peace of mind escaped;

Granted wishes at home, world beyond betrayed

Unaware being watched, you and your clan strayed;

The Devoted said:

One rarely finds someone filled with pride for being just. All feel cheated and victimized by the society.

For petty gains you resort to unfair means and try to outsmart the deserving. You offer bribes to gain favours.

You changed your nature and your views to suit your needs and thought you deceived the society undetected. Thus you deceived yourself.

You thought your deeds would get you happiness by trying to fill your barren life with the luxuries of the world. When exposed, you were disturbed and lost your sleep.

You amassed wealth for self and your family without any concern for the society. You thought no one took stock of your sins and continued to commit crime.

Fed a greedy family, that you bred with lust

Greased palms and self, slipped to bite the dust;

Demanded bribe of you, traitors you christened

Corrupt their character, wish you had questioned;

Thus your growth set an ideal, for fellow foes to emulate

To set scores with brethren, corrupt minds you stimulate;

Poked one another you all, home of trust you bored

Jumping high in glory, dishonesty beneath springboard;

Tread on weaker shoulders, forcing up submission

Gain strength from weakness, Dear Devotee's mission."

You strived hard to provide your family all the comforts but resorting to means not approved by your own society. You made your journey smooth but slipped morally.

Those who demanded bribes of you were traitors of the society. You blamed them but towed their line showing helplessness. You should have refrained from malice.

You succeeded in making money and inspired others to follow you. Those who felt exploited found it easy to bribe and progress in a corrupt society.

You created a chain reaction of corruption and looted one another by losing mutual trust. Betrayal and dishonesty propelled you to make fortune.

The weak were forced to give in to the demands of the powerful. The strong ones planned to gain strength by draining the resources of the poor and needy.

CHAPTER 17

THE PEOPLE'S AGENDA

"One against the many, the hapless ones looted

Part with one's fortunes, or standby to be booted;

Testing time is penury, honesty if leased

Will at will mortgaged, asking to be fleeced;

Wanders one in search, hoping for a job

In by-lanes of misfortune, traps set to rob;

A future full in blossom, demands one to invest

An Invite for humbugs, hovering on to infest;

Sick of sickness many, they hanker for a cure

Lay in wait to trap, your fellow being for sure;

There are many dishonest people waiting to trap the gullible fellow citizens. If the gullible ones do not pay up the ransom they will be deprived of their rightful worth.

One who is poor and in need faces the test of honesty. If one succumbs to the compulsions, then exploitation is inevitable.

The jobless are desperate to get employment and in that state they fail to realize the dangers lurking in the form of charlatans to rob them.

The naïve one is lured to invest in return of a bright future. Many get cheated as they easily believe their fellow citizens who promise them a fortune.

The underprivileged and the unfortunate ones want to get rid of the curse of poverty and are ready to get trapped by the cheats.

Exist hands to help, a clan of friendly neighbour
Should soul next-door weep, or grieve at love's labour?

Hoping for ways to mend, and farewell to bumpy ride
Take the honest ways within, or masses for a ride;

Nature's agents healthy, share and gift you health
Agents grow healthy, that serve the people filth;

A place to hold your name, a hut to call your home
They landed on your land, you left on streets to roam;

Body laden with weight of vice, you cried to be heard
Muffled by hands like your own, voice lost in the herd."

There are still good Samaritans in the society who care for the neighbour in grief and would venture out to lend a helping hand.

The one in pain has the choice to emulate the virtuous and lead a clean life or follow the forbidden route and fleece fellow being and grow rich fast.

All citizens are provided with resources to grow and progress. To disseminate fairly is the duty of Nature, whereas, to deprive unfairly is the selfish human creature.

You try hard and struggle all life to settle your family to live peacefully. The selfish fellow being robs you of your rightful place and leaves you homeless.

You and your likes bore the brunt of injustice and tried to raise voice against it. The criminal elements of the society suppressed your cries and put you down.

CHAPTER 18

VICTIMS OF SELF DECEPTION

Said the Devoted:

"Beams after loot, a face soaked in piety

Real ones left out, in base, collective dacoity;

Calls the commoner, greed's devil set to eat you

Win I shall your wealth and surely defeat you;

All see I prey, all see I predators

Barring a few naïve, all clever traitors;

Each vying with another, fears no law or prison

Self-morphing selfish, blaming fellow citizen;

Me nor my clan, subverts one's honesty

Dealings in your kind, who lacks sincerity;

The Devoted said:

Each one looks so pious and clean in spite of the shady deals one indulges in. Those who work sincerely are ill paid and the slimy creatures mint money.

Common people like you pamper their greed and fool the gullible to satisfy their wants. It is the commoner who robs a fellow commoner.

I find all to be either the victims or the victors in this game of self-deception and mutual plunder. The situation decides the role played by the commoner.

The fierce competition among the people for survival makes them selfish. They in turn blame others for the corruption and lawlessness in the society.

Highly placed elite people like us are not always to be blamed for the perils of the common people. If people are honest with one another, the mutual loot would cease.

Ruler call I myself, surely don't rule the mind

Honest fellow subject, a creature rare to find;

Cast in different molds, you switch role

You frame your clone, and acquit on parole;

Shackled by petty issues, rooted to the ground

Constrained your vision, to watch all around;

Crafty moves you make, to fellow being indict

Frosty eyes see no future, hawkish eyes predict;

Soaring above you, view I acts so brazen

Welcome grief unseen, waiting beyond horizon."

I may be elected to govern but I don't govern the thoughts of the people. I may make laws for all but very rarely find law abiding, sincere citizens.

You, the common citizen, change roles so easily and so often to escape the law and if need be, implicate your fellow being in your criminal act.

Your personal need and troubles prevent you from seeing beyond the horizon. You keep yourself blissfully unaware of the larger problems around you.

You use your clever mind to avoid being caught and in turn punish others. In such acts of selfishness, you fail to see the harm you do to the society.

I can visualize the outcome of the mean acts of yours and your brethren. The misery and misfortune that befalls you is your creation.

CHAPTER 19

THE AGENDA OF DEMOCRACY

Said the Devoted:

"Leader the power center, wields the power **of the people**

Pearl cast away as pebble, priceless vote **of the people;**

Strength in number I collect, gifted **by the people**

My victory a royal burden, to be lifted **by the people;**

I toil day and night, due promises **for the people**

Worship of their lord brings, nemesis **for the people;**

Worshiped do I get, for sworn promises to keep

They tear benign hearts, and deny me tears to weep;

Expectant of social change, power in me they vested

Resistant of own change, for personal gain invested;

The Devoted said:

In a democracy the leaders enjoy the power vested in them by the trusting subjects. People do not realize the power of their vote and squander away their power.

The strength and victory of the leader is in the number of votes collected in the elections. I, the public servant, am put on a pedestal and treated like a king.

I make all efforts to keep the promises I made before the elections. People make us demigods and by expecting us to take away all their troubles and sufferings increase them further.

I, once a commoner, am worshiped on becoming a leader. The commoners continue to exploit one another and expect me to not oppose the treason committed by them.

They vote me to power to eradicate the social evil that they themselves perpetuate. They resist all attempts to change by bribing me for their personal gains.

They strung the leader, people sole authority
Puppet in hands aplenty, hunting for polarity;

A few freaks left out, most nurture corrupt intents
Voter pleads honest, the leader's honour dents;

Swarms of cunning hover, pester till obliged
Mean dreams of hordes, demand to be realized;

Convoy of malpractice, rides smooth without a hitch
Finds honest cart of labour, at every step a ditch;

Tall promises of my folks, undone and forgotten
Need you not know how, fruits of hope get rotten."

People elect the leader of their choice and the ones closer to the leader coerce the leader to fulfill all their demands. They still expect the leader to be fair to all.

Barring a few sincere and rightful demands, a majority are illegal and unjust. The subjects still feign honesty and curse the leader for the corruption in the society.

Herds of these selfish followers pressurize and plead to be gratified. Each one expects that the leader is obliged to heed to their unfair demands.

Those who grease the palms of the ones in power get their share of loot. Those who tread the path of truth and honesty face many hurdles.

The promises that we make to the people before the elections are relegated by majority of selfish people and the rest hope in vain for a better governance.

CHAPTER 20

LEADER OF LEADERS

Skeptic mind of Devotee, puts the Devoted to test

The Leadership puzzle, let's not doubts to rest;

Said the Devotee:

"Social leaders sprinkled liberally among the masses

Half empty sees some, others half-filled glasses;

Leader of faith unite, to divide naive believers

Love own, others to disown, fiery sermon delivers;

Chasing goals sky high, the leadership corporate

Ends justify the means, lets morality evaporate;

Putting brain and brawn together, seen leader in defense

All is fair in love for war, dare no one take offense;

The Devotee still has many queries about the different kinds of leadership and the methods of governance.

The Devotee said:

There are many people who want to bring a change in the society by doing social work. Their efforts seem convincing for some people, but others suspect them.

Religious leaders propagate their views and force the followers to believe in their own faith and exclude other faiths.

Leaders in business have the sole aim of furthering their financial interests by employing fair but most of the time unfair means.

The military leadership uses both physical and mental strength to overpower the enemy. They display absolute authority in seeing everything fair in the art of war.

Alien and marooned, all make leader of morals
Humanoid none mimics, to praise none quarrels;

Leaders of all hue, at your feet prostrate
Magic wand concealed, troubled souls remonstrate;"

Said the Devoted:
"Magic wand of ruler, at hand nor remote
My power rests in you, the all-powerful vote;

Bestows on me power, blesses me with vice
Holy souls than me, why line up for advice;

Ones that pleaded for your vote, you turn into pleaders
One who promised to serve, became leader of leaders."

The flag bearers of morality find few followers and are avoided by the commoners. But at the same time the people do not hesitate to praise the moral leaders.

All these leaders are your subjects and are to follow your diktats. I wonder what secret you hold to lord over all other leaders.

Said the Devoted:

I do not have any magical trick to govern the people and the various leaders. I enjoy the power due to the votes cast by the people.

People empower me and then expect me to oblige them in all their ill deeds. They think they are honest, but they hanker for my advice.

Me and my clan begged for your votes with folded hands to serve the society as loyal servants, but you turned us into demigods and worshiped us.

CHAPTER 21

THE BITTER YOU – THE BETTER YOU

"Behold! the commoner, the idol of reverence

Demand for self, armed with indifference;

When fellow beings suffer, they hide in a shell

A taste of bitter pill and heaven turns to hell;

Each weave for self, safe and cozy cocoon

Insured for life they hope, face Bitter truth soon;

Asks the suffering one, other's whereabouts

Not one noble helps, locked in verbal bouts;

Turned a blind eye, when hell broke loose

Cries of help unheard, nothing feared to lose;

Watch the traits of the commoner while dealing with self-interest and social responsibilities.

People do not bother about the sufferings of the fellow citizens in trouble but cry hoarse when trouble troubles them.

Each one wants a safe haven for self and the family. They do not realize that they too would face the harsh realities of living in a society.

When the one in trouble calls for help, none steps forward. The same people would debate ceaselessly for social justice and good governance.

Most people hesitate to venture out and extend a helping hand to the needy. They avoid inconvenience when they have nothing at stake.

Hoped saviors rushed to help, but lips offered sympathy

Self not cared for, they curse the world's apathy;

Soldier risks own life, to prevail over the foes

Guards a nation asleep, fends a million woes;

Two faces of coin, the one suffers the Bitter you

Friend of fortune, on the other side the Better you;

Cast in same elements, cursed not to meet

One face turns cold, when the other feels the heat;

Turn around slowly, each has a different frame

Flick into a spin and both appear the same.

When in trouble they expect others to help them. But like all others they too get to hear only words of sympathy and then they curse the people for being indifferent.

True warriors risk their lives to safeguard the interests of the fellow citizens. In the presence of such guardians, nations all over the world sleep peacefully.

Each citizen has to see the two faces of self. The one that faces injustice is the Bitter one. The other face that furthers injustice is the Better one.

Both faces are of the same individual but when one is exposed to injustice, the other face looks the other side.

A rare occasion of misfortune does not bring the two faces together. Frequent brawls with injustice compel the faces to face each other and the truth.

CHAPTER 22

THE BITTER YOU – A CALL FOR MATERNAL CARE

Spoke the Devoted to the victim of vice:

"We all were children and for children do we care

I share your lamentations on health and family welfare;

Cry must all at birth, none born with a smile

Music to all who hear, welcome to world of guile;

Banished for one life, to grow in size and number

Jolted out of sleep, a pure heavenly slumber;

Sans vision and wisdom, you grew up on feelings

World at large uncaring, motherly touch for healing;

If voice could you, infant thoughts, would blame creator supreme

Sleep for ever and never leave, the benign world of dream;

The Devoted said:

We all are aware of the hardship we faced as children and would work together to care for the young generation. I share with you the plaint of the parents in pain.

The cry of a newborn is music to the parents and relatives who welcome the child into a world full of hurdles for the tiny life to battle.

Life grows and propagates as children are born in a troubled world. They leave the safety of the mother's womb where they slept peacefully.

You had no eyes and wisdom for comfort in the disturbing surroundings. You totally depended on the maternal care in the absence of basic health care facilities.

You would curse the creator for exposing you to a ruthless and uncaring world if you could voice your thoughts and would have preferred to stay in your dreamland.

Birth not your choice but you deserved better treatment

I share your lamentations on woman and child development;

Tiny forehead frowned, beady nostrils flared

Expressed anguish at birth, mother child uncared;

Safe secure journey from mother to motherland

Air scant to breath, space too crowded to stand;

All too busy in business, who should care for the child

You lamented cursed midwife, on childbirth in the wild;

In crowd of mother's expectant, you took birth in a mob

Child cried the pain out and mother hid her sob."

You had no right to choose your birthplace but certainly had a right to better facilities for your development. I share your plaint in this regard.

You sniffed the air for the first time and experienced the harsh reality of living in this world. You expressed discomfort on getting exposed to a hostile environment.

Your birth was maybe without any trouble for you and your mother, but as you arrived, you felt the air heavy and place around you, crowded and noisy.

You found the caretakers too busy to attend to your needs as there were others to be cared for. You cursed the one who brought and welcomed you into this world.

With many others you took birth in a crowded hospital without proper facilities. You cried out in protest but your mother like many others hid her suffering.

CHAPTER 23

THE BITTER YOU – A CALL FOR BASIC NEEDS

"Deprived children unequal, millions stand as proof

I share your lamentations on four walls and a roof;

Clusters of nests concrete, one named your home

Breeze life giving barred, blood sucking creatures roam;

Felt pinch of heat, as the blinding lights went out

Where on Earth is this hell, in wails alone could you shout?

Din and dirt of society, beyond visual horizon

Ear and nose bore the brunt, of noise and airy poison;

A home for homecoming, a puff of life deprived

Dream of a lesser being, poverty's child arrived;

Many children like you are deprived of a shelter and are a proof of the injustice meted to them. I share with you the woes in a poor dwelling.

Houses built in confined areas formed concrete jungles where even breeze was cut out. The hut that was your home was infested with blood sucking pests.

In the absence of electric supply, you were left out in the dark and hot place to suffer. You cried wondering in which hellish place on Earth you descended.

You could not see the unfriendly surroundings that the society offered you, but your tiny ears and nose were subjected to silent torture.

You were deprived of homely surroundings when you arrived. You dream of a healthy and welcoming home but were deprived, being born of poor parents.

Well before your birth, were sown misery's seeds

I share your lamentations on life's basic needs;

Grew in motherland, that weaned you from mother

One made you weep in hunger, when hungry cried the other;

Crop aplenty to harvest, pods filled to spill

Haves bask in the Sun, have-nots feel the chill;

Famine in land of plenty, curse the guardians of nation

Blame the great governance, that gifted mass starvation;

Promise to lead through storm, left your dreams shattered

The Favoured draped in silk, rest stripped and tattered."

The actions that caused your sufferings were taken by the society much before you were born. I share your grief on the deprivation of basic human needs.

The motherland in which you set your feet took away all the comfort that your mother provided before your birth. It left you hungry and your mother crying.

There was no dearth of food in the state's granary, yet you were hungry. Those who had the resources enjoyed and left you starving.

The indifference and carelessness of a few created famine like situation for the poor. Poor distribution and bad governance of the nation made people to starve.

Those who ensured the people of a safe journey abandoned them. The subjects who earned favour through wrong deeds sailed safe and the rest were marooned.

CHAPTER 24

THE BITTER YOU – A CALL FROM THE COUNTRYSIDE

"From times beyond memory, mutely bore the yoke

I share your lamentations on state of the rural folk;

Raised in rustic lanes, wrapped in dusty blanket

A few moments of fest, slums turning to banquet;

Scores of generations dreamt, of life in a lovely city

Crores of wealth showered, made you symbol of pity.

Promises tall to keep, to brighten gloom of the rural

Fortunes flowed to preach, bloomed sermons floral;

Bodies born numerous, to deliver rural justice

Countryside governance, no serious job-just tease;

The rustic has been toiling and suffering from ages without voicing their protest. I share your pain on the state of the rural populace,

The surroundings in the villages have always been dusty and unclean. Occasional festive events bring a temporary glitter in the otherwise unkempt hamlets.

From generations the rural people wished to bring the pomp of the cities to the villages. Large amount of money changed hands to change the pitiable state.

People in power promised to bring urban life to the villages. Money meant for the progress of the rural stayed in the cities and only hollow speeches reached them.

Numerous organizations sprang up to transform the villages. Majority of them intended to make money for self. Rural governance was never taken seriously.

Bloom of knowledge potent, urban mind's lancer

I share your lamentations on stunting rural cancer;

Scholars praised knowledge, since bygone stone age

Yet out of reach for you, shackled in urban bondage;

Subtle knowhow seeps, deep in brain's tiny fold

Caged as mute witness, rural miseries untold;

Learning, right to learning, just a fancy slogan

Might that rules the mind, still the rusty gun;

Mark of civilization, that built a great nation

In rustic desert you chased, a mirage of education."

Knowledge is the weapon of the people living in the cities. The cancer of illiteracy hampers the growth of the people residing in the rural areas. I share your pain on the state of education in the villages.

Education has been a necessity for human development since ancient times. Villages have been deprived of academic facilities that are available in the towns.

The knowledge that can make way in the tiny folds of the human brain finds no access into the villages. The minds of the rural folk are blocked causing untold suffering for centuries.

The propaganda of Right to Education remains on paper. In practice, might alone rules the people.

Education has created mighty nations and civilization. Humanity has progressed due to the flow of information and technology. In villages, however, proper education is a dream.

CHAPTER 25

THE BITTER YOU – A CALL FROM ETHER TO EARTH

"The learned foresee, predict the zodiac signs

I share your lamentations on betrayal of science;

Curious brains turned, science into celestial boon

Heavenly life on Earth, a dwelling on the moon;

Earthy creatures thanked the gods, feeling honed

Echoed the world around, age of science had dawned;

Free and fair governance, science of politics taught

To serve the downtrodden, loyal servants fought;

Fed all on promises, science in communication

Left in the lurch, beleaguered child of starvation;

The erudite scholars study and plan their future. The astrologers study the heavens and predict the future. I share your pain on the use and abuse of science.

The honest disciples of science made good use of their knowledge to the benefit of the masses. Science turned out to be a boon for the Earthlings who think of populating the Moon.

Humans thank the gods for bestowing the celestial knowledge on them and sharpen their intellect. Humans herald the era of science and technology that has changed their lives.

Similarly, the science of Politics teaches to manage and maintain the administrative set up in a fair and just manner. The political aspirants quarrel to serve the weak and the poor and fight for their rights.

They feed the people with tall promises to transform their lives with the gifts of science. The expectant masses remain hungry as the rulers usurp their share.

With science omnipotent, Ether and Earth cements
I share your lamentations on scarce healthy elements;

Sniffed the air acrid, the infant nostrils flared
Tiny ears twitched, for countless hooters blared;

Settled future's hope, in cradle of emotions
Rocked the life benign, hands of commotion;

Caution, the word, when mother offered water
Pray not trust aqua, life of nature's daughter;

Precious minerals sipped, to stand the baby tall
Cashing on parent's peril, mammon's morals fall."

The power of science has made seemingly impossible feats possible. Human species has conquered space and has traversed beyond. This progress is at a price. I share your pain on the abuse of the natural resources.

The life-giving air is polluted and a newly born sniffs the poisonous air. The noise levels have reached high and are unbearable to the infant. We are unable to offer a habitable, healthy environment to our children.

The future of our young ones rests in a worried and insecure parent. The parents are themselves not sure of what the new generation will beget.

Water, the prime medium of life, seems unsafe for the infant. Parents dread to offer contaminated water lest the infant is harmed.

Food required to sustain life and grow healthy and strong is adulterated by fellow humans for personal gains. They reap high profits on others' predicament.

CHAPTER 26

THE BITTER YOU – A CALL FOR POWER AND ENERGY

"With bias towards none, heavenly energies shower

I share your lamentations on divested energy, power;

Power to all granted, a few chosen wired

Quite a few shunned, the turbines lay tired;

You found blessed powered, ever on stately walk

Burned midnight oil, you are in for a shock;

Daybreak saw you asleep, overworks the eye lens

Night kept you awake, in roar of deafening silence;

Fought for drops of fuel, to light up gloomy lives

Battle on dried up wells, with no claws or knives;

Nature gifts its store of energy without any undue favour towards any particular class or race. The power and energy generated by humans gets delivered to the privileged class and the poor rural class is deprived of it. I share your pain on the deprivation of basic facilities like power to the underprivileged.

Enough electrical power is available to light up the urban as well as the rural homes. The chosen ones get uninterrupted supply by draining the source but the needy face frequent power cuts.

You find the lucky ones enjoying the continuous flow of life current. It is indeed shocking for those who are not wired to the grid and have to toil in the dark.

You sleep in the daytime due to strenuous work at night. The silence of the dark night is also too loud for you to sleep peacefully.

Majority of people like you have to struggle for every drop of oil you use to light the lamp. Without any kind of help you fight over the drying supplies of fuel that come your way.

Humble hands that feed, the hands that cut get bold

I share your lamentations on guts digesting green gold;

Nature has abundant, for creatures one and all

Humans desire nature, to serve at beck and call;

Reckless ways nay unnatural, left the mother ravished

A million hands to tear, a few more to mend she wished;

Carpet at their feet, a canopy overhead green

Flowery branches in fruition, gentle love birds preen;

Safe haven for predation, now feline dread the forest

Till homely woods denuded, will human race not rest."

The farmers that produce grains and feed the people have humility and responsibility. The poachers who cut trees indiscriminately get bolder with each criminal act. I share your pain on the plunder of natural resources.

Nature provides for the needs of all the creatures on the planet and maintains balance between the producers and the consumers. Humans on the other hand exploit nature, thanks to the progress made in inventing machines that assist them to plunder nature.

The consumption of nature's produce without tending to the demands of Mother Nature disrupts the healing process of nature. We need more people to mend the damage being done by a majority of people.

Nature provides us with all the comforts of home. There is beauty in abundance all around. The flora and fauna exist for all animals to feed and grow.

The forests were a heaven for the animal to hunt for food. The intrusion of human beings has scared even the wild beasts. The greed of the humans will not allow them to stop till the forests disappear from the planet.

CHAPTER 27

THE BITTER YOU – A CALL FOR RIGHT CHEMISTRY

"Base of all emotions, root of human understanding

I share your lamentations on skewed chemical bonding;

Knocked you out of sleep, odour prickly pungent

Breezed out puff of fresh air, some humanoids negligent;

Universe near and far, evolved in chemical soup

Affinity, the booster of life, gifted to favoured group;

Elements playing games, species found no bound

Catalysts human minds, saw their vows compound;

Tailored nature's design, human innovation

Set in chemical riot, you called suffocation;

All emotions and feelings of the living world depend on a delicate chemical balance in the brain. Human understanding of the world is also the outcome of that chemical bonding. I share your pain on the turmoil in that chemical bonding.

Air pollution caused irritation in humans and has hampered their comfortable living. The poisoning of the atmosphere is the result of some utterly negligent people who never bothered to acknowledge the harm they did to nature.

The universe with all its matter, living or non-living evolved from the interaction of different elements. Liking of some matter to other evolved more specialized beings.

This interplay of elements and compounds produced diverse life forms. The more evolved human being interfered with the natural process causing tremendous irreparable loss.

Humans manipulated nature to suit their requirement and altered the natural processes. The pollution of all-natural resources is the outcome of the abuse of human technology.

Voyage of matter organic, set minds on new course
I share your lamentations on wasted human resource;

All lesser lives survive, a task seeming immense
Precious human life, a resource for super humans;

You make super humans, of puny mortal beings
Lament over future, a fruit of wrong doings;

Bred and cared by them, to become cannon fodder
Submit to their will, my brethren obey their order;

They market human resource, as items of consumption
Value human values least, and hope for redemption."

Migration of people to distant places made some to think of it as a business opportunity. I share your pain on the treatment of human beings as being commodities.

Every human being fights a battle for survival which in itself is a daunting task. The powerful and privileged ones treat others as a resource for them to exploit.

You consider the rich and powerful like me as superhuman. They too are human beings with human follies. You worship them and pay the price in the form of mental subjugation.

The underprivileged are fed just so much as to be able to serve the exploiters without any protest. The weak surrender to the powerful without a fight.

The rich, powerful, and erudite, all treat fellow humans as commodities and desire to buy them for a price. Nevertheless, they desire to build a progressive society.

CHAPTER 28

THE BITTER YOU – A CALL FOR RIGHT LIVELIHOOD

"Blood, sweat and sinews, eager to feed the being

I share your lamentations on right to earn a living;

Driven out of nest, to fetch a few morsels

To satiate hunger eternal, bane of all mortals;

Job for hands befitting, prayers too many to heed

A hundred hands to labour, a million mouths to feed;

You pray, plead or punch, poor fellow struggler

Seen one well employed, a crafty little juggler;

For bribe, beauty, barter, landed service public

Sleazy private market, needs honeyed lips to lick;

Everyone seems eager to find a job for sustenance. They are ready to labour hard and sweat or bleed for it. I share your pain on the state of employment and the right to earn livelihood.

All are drawn into the open to earn and feed their families. The need to satisfy one's hunger is a never-ending struggle.

People in great numbers, qualified or otherwise, pray for a decent employment. The earning members are far outnumbered by the mouths they have to feed.

The honest job seeker keeps struggling for a job. The dishonest ones bribe their way to a good post.

Those who are willing to use unfair means get selected in the coveted government services. The private services demand beauty, sweet talks, and sycophancy.

Search for job spanned, length and breadth of the nation

I share your lamentations on highway to destination;

A step out of home, the road turns to altar

The road siphons life, the builder molten tar;

Smooth ride a dream, bones, muscles snap

Many breakers you take, law breakers a nap;

In search of few bites, on roads you bite the dust

Wait for one to pave the way, with intent clean and just;

Heaps of curses piled up, and dug up several graves

On roads of misery several, for road untrodden one craves."

People like you traveled far and wide for a job. The traveler found the rides too inconvenient and bone breaking, thanks to the poor roads. I share your pain on the state of the roads.

Many people lose their lives as they step out of their safe homes. The roads are killing fields on which many lives are lost. The commuters sacrifice their lives and the builders, the quality of construction.

All dream to ride on smooth roads without any trouble. The roads offer jolts and shake you as you confront potholes, but the lawbreakers enjoy oblivious to the troubles of the people.

In search of livelihood one roams on the dusty roads hoping for someone to display a rare act of honesty and build good roads to the destination.

You curse the government and the builders for constructing bad roads and in the process lose several lives on the road. You wish to travel on roads of your dreams.

CHAPTER 29

THE BITTER YOU – A CALL FOR JUDICIOUS PLANNING

"Rich or poor, but each, progress monetary compares

I share your lamentations on dismal fiscal affairs;

For you the valued voter, we drew up grand dreams

In desert it snowed, grew oasis, lawns and streams;

Few see the daylight, Sun upon them never dawns

Hutment dreams nightmares, in palace spring up lawns.

Millions swarm around, nibbling valued treasure

Quenching each appetite, filling one's measure;

Business in benevolence, benefits none benign

The evil turn saviors, to serve souls divine;

Everyone compares the amount of money earned and decides one's success based on how wealthy one grew. I share your pain on the financial inequality in life.

We the leaders, plan big projects for the benefit of the people. We claim to spend huge amounts on providing for the needs and luxuries of life. The dreams of the people are never fulfilled.

A very few projects are completed. The money shown to be spent on them is never put to good use. The needy and poor for whom the money was meant remain poor but the ones who planned get richer.

There exist millions of such project managers and workers who usurp public funds. Instead of utilizing the funds for the benefit of the society, they fill their treasure chests.

Social work carried out by the charlatans to serve the people is one way of cheating and a means to get rich fast. The fraudulent pose as saviors but the ones who are genuinely honest and divine are left unattended and unrewarded.

Swindled day or night, no hand to dispense peace

I share your lamentations on lame law and justice;

Haunted by a million, the feeble turn to the jury

Jury's hands in shackles, to prevent balm injury;

You dread to default, dotting dealings fair

Watch the wolves wallow, basking in the lair;

At will they torment, unmindful goons trespass

Every legal crossing, find lawful ones impasse;

With decayed deaf ears, legal battles fought

For decades hearings last, till justice is bought."

People are cheated and looted all the time but are unable to get justice when they complain. I share your pain on the denial of justice to the hapless victim.

Charlatans lay in wait to swindle the gullible. The victims expect the judicial machinery to dispense justice. The legal fraternity finds it difficult to do justice to their duty and alleviate the sufferings of the people.

The honest commoners are afraid of the law and steer clear of the troubles of litigations. Those who know the tricks to bypass the laws enjoy without any fear.

The criminals torture the simple ones by resorting to illegal means. The fair player finds hurdles at every step.

The pleadings of the righteous victim fall on deaf ears. The legal cases are stretched for years and the one who pays handsomely wins.

CHAPTER 30

THE BITTER YOU – A CALL FOR IDENTITY

"Mutated to diverse forms, the man-made sculpture

I share your lamentations on erosion of culture;

Bounty of nature, for every creature's taking

Gift of culture select, human society's making;

Values that you held high, slighted, booted, spurned

Fallen from grace unworthy, laurels lofty earned;

Winds sinister sweep away, culture pods, ideals

Weeds diseased planted, lapping rich minerals;

Many a gallant fall, for phantom culture war

Harvest of ethically dead, the waiting vultures far;

The human form, though the same anatomically, takes various forms depending on Tradition, Culture and Geography. I share your pain on the erosion of cultural values.

The resources of nature are the same all over the world, but civilizations differ due to cultural practices unique to the human species.

The values and ideals that are cherished and respected in one culture are laughed at in another. People who are despised in one culture are venerated and worshiped in another.

Every nation fears invasion of foreign culture to destroy it's own. The traditional thinkers blame the unethical and immoral foreign values for the degeneration of the younger generation.

Those who deliberately expose the younger generation to foreign culture with intent to start a cultural war between generations stand benefited. The ones who fight to preserve their identity and their cultural heritage come to harm.

Stature of mighty players, reduced to a puny pawn

I share your lamentations on failed brain and brawn;

A fair game assured, to showcase your skills

Nepotism's detour denied, a slot that talent fills;

Tried your hand in games, that gave you shock

Put shoulder to cog, the boats you steer rock;

Battle to win a cup, fishing in troubled waters

Cups and medals lost, tired sons and daughters;

Play by the rules, and sink to deep trenches

Play by the rulers, a leper but prize wrenches."

People with skill and will to work hard to succeed lose the battle due to unfair play. I share your pain on the failure of the deserving.

Fairness and transparency are promised and claimed in all competitions. The talented and honest competitors are assured of a berth ruling out any favoritism.

People like you are in for surprise when you actually participate in the game of survival. They play honestly but soon realize that the game is not being played as per rules.

Attempt to win seems to be fraught with bias and frustration. The struggle against nepotism soon tires the fair player who gains nothing, though deserving.

One who goes by the rules is unlikely to succeed and finally will meet failure and frustration. One who sides with the people who set the rules may not be worthy at all but becomes an assured winner.

CHAPTER 31

THE BITTER YOU – A CALL FOR SELF EXPRESSION

"Canvas, theater, sheet, or street, rules the street smart

I share your lamentations on dilution of sacred art;

Dreams that the soul cast, close to your heart

Put forth for adoring eyes, shut tight on art;

Let down by own folk, sulking under betrayal

Skillful soul's sensitive heart, bore silent trial;

Priceless jewels cut and carved, squandered as pebbles

Many a blessed artists' pride, burst like soap bubbles;

With art penury but runs, for few honour the prize

Alas! For lack of patrons, you paid the price;

In all media of expression, be it painting, acting, writing or oration, the crafty ones seem to excel. I share your pain on the exclusion of real artists from limelight.

The artist puts all the creativity and hard work in the work of art, hoping to please the art lovers and catch the attention of the jury. The judges expect something extra to gratify them, turning a blind eye to the art itself.

The honest artist feels betrayed by fellow artists who resort to sycophancy to win accolades. One, being a true artist, not programmed to fight back, suffers in silence.

A real work of art does not get recognition and a place of honour in the art gallery. The poor artist's dream of being appreciated for the skill and hard work is shattered due to dishonest judges.

Art and artists are not honoured and rewarded adequately. There are very few people who give an unbiased judgment and honour art purely on merit. In the bargain, art and the artist suffer.

Media, movie, television, for projection in harness

I share your lamentations on social unawareness;

Pleasure, love, knowledge, spread as revelation

On vehicles of media, to enrich new generation;

Percolating fissures, exposing truth and lies

Unceasing rain of events, euphoria soon dies;

Events doctored in frames; truth willfully concealed

Media a powerful tool, a weapon falsely perceived;

Hoped to deliver justice, print in chips or spools

You learnt media speaks, for one that on it rules."

The omnipresent audio-visual media with an omniscient image of itself displays truths and lies. I share your pain on the misinformation and the curbing of awareness of the people.

The media disseminates information on events that bring joy, pleasure, and wisdom to the people. People feel happier, wiser, and well equipped in dealing with their problems.

The media describes events in detail and in a repetitive manner to reach the very core of human mind. The overdose and over exposure of events to the senses soon numbs them, cluttering the minds of the people.

Facts are cleverly manipulated to serve the interests of the media owner. Media, a powerful tool to educate the people and bring clarity in thought, is used as a weapon to frame innocents or worship a villain.

As technology progressed, one hoped that the media was unbiased and showed events as recorded, displaying transparency. The truth is that media divulges information that the owner dictates.

CHAPTER 32

THE BETTER YOU – A CAUTION ON MATERNAL CARE

Spoke the Devoted to the voice of vice:

"Blessed with children, but for children not you care

I share not your loot in health and family welfare;

Tunes you set unheard, for parenthood to dance

Legs not adept falter, to fleece present a chance;

Each child born to live, a life time of opportunity

For you to loot the parent, for them life's continuity;

Sobs of mother, wails of the child, ears deafened quashed

Pain of fellow creatures, for pleasure you encashed;

Reaped harvest to full bloom, on another's misfortune

Mother and child suffered, among vultures opportune;

The Devoted thus addressed the one who practiced vice:

You too are a parent, but you ignored the other parents and did not look after the needs of their children. I do not share your spoils in the family welfare schemes.

People like you made other parents to fulfill your unjust demands. Those who failed to comply were denied the care they deserved.

Every child has a right to live healthily and make good use of the opportunities for a successful life. For you they were an opportunity to fleece their parents.

Devoid of basic needs and facilities, the mother and the child cried, but it had no effect on your ears that were deafened by the jingle of wealth. Their pain became your pleasure.

Your harvests came to full bloom and enriched your life. The parents and the children suffered pain due to incessant pecking by vultures like you.

Honesty not your choice, they deserved better treatment
I share not your loot in woman and child development;

Stocks named for children, went down the wrong lane
Enriched your greedy brood, nourished demonic brains;

Warm hands caring froze, shivered in the corrupting cold
Rugs you pecked to rags, dime a dozen you sold;

Deprived them of space, herded them in a mob
The rich born in poverty, fellow citizens thus rob;

Laid your hands on riches, carrying your job with stealth
Siphoned neighbour's stock, sucked on sibling's health."

You employed dishonest means to make a fortune by usurping the facilities that the parents and the wards deserved. I do not share your spoils in the women and child development schemes.

Funds and facilities meant for the people were diverted to your den where it fed your children. Feed bought for the innocents fed the wicked ones.

The clothing for the poor parents to warm themselves and protect their child were pecked and picked by you and sold to make money.

The space marked for them you sold to others for a price. The ones who were provided, lived in clustered habitat among the mobs of deprived fellow citizens.

You silently laid your hands on the belongings of your neighbours and brethren. You robbed them of their rights to become rich.

CHAPTER 33

THE BETTER YOU – A CAUTION ON BASIC NEEDS

"You erased the thin line, between living and warfare

I share not your loot in health and family welfare;

Blocks for housing brethren, blocked their way to home

Raised your home instead, in a day was built your Rome;

Sans light and breeze, feet stumbled and sweat showered

Energy defied nature, from low to high it powered;

Tasked to clean the din, turned blind eye to squalour

Amassed wealth out of filth, a testimony to your valour;

Weak, tired, disabled, you ensured stayed deprived

Wounded and suffering, on them your fortune thrived;

You and people like you made one another's life a battle for survival.
I do not share your spoils in health and family welfare.

The building blocks meant to build your fellow citizens' houses,
blocked their way to home. Whereas they waited for ever for a house,
you raised your house in no time.

In the absence of electricity people groped in the dark and bore the
heat and the cold. Contrary to the laws of nature where energy flows
from higher to lower level, the power was diverted from the poor to
the rich.

It was your responsibility to maintain and clean living spaces. You
neglected your duty and spent the money for your welfare.

You looted the share of the weak and tired people and made a fortune
on their misfortune.

Lamb in nature doomed, crafty wolf succeeds

I share not your loot in life's basic needs;

Crop aplenty in fields, loaded pods of grain

Bundles of wealth for you, ryot's labour vain;

A handful that they wished, for every morsel fought

Tons stacked up in your chests, uncared, left to rot;

Braving all odds for you, smiling laboured ryot

Fair demand of labour's child, you declared a riot;

Strong lives the son of soil, you made them look funny

Did heart that bled revolt, when you were minting money."

The simple ones at heart lost the battle for survival to cunning people like you. I do not share your spoils in the battle for basic needs.

The farmer worked hard to produce good crop. It ensured hefty gains for you. The ryot returned empty handed and slept on empty stomach.

The poor wished food enough to fend hunger. You had plenty of grains in your stores, but you were too greedy to share with them. You left it to rot in the stores.

The farmers toiled day and night to raise crop for you. You denied them their share. When they demanded it, you called it revolt.

The strong farmers worked in the fields with a smile without complaining. You slighted their labour. They never mocked you when you were busy making money.

CHAPTER 34

THE BETTER YOU – A CAUTION FROM THE COUNTRYSIDE

"Under the strain of greed, the umbilical cord broke

I share not your loot from betrayal of rural folk;

Parked in cozy couches, steered dreamy projects ambitious

Rustic beauty tailored to park, for pricey fruits delicious;

You sang for them lullaby, to sleep through poverty

Made fortune till shaken, dream-landers faced reality;

None came to senses, truth knocking they nap

Moments to treasure rolled by, you drew Utopian map;

They stumble over treasure, troves lost in paradise

You ornate your life divine, the poor dreamer dies;

The lifeline of the rural people was severed to starve the rural folk and enrich the urban lot. I do not share your spoils in the looting of the naïve village folk.

You designed grand projects from your comfortable offices and homes for the suffering villages. You planned to transform the villages into beautiful parks and orchard that would finally bear fruits for you.

The villagers were unaware of your plans and continued to dream of a beautiful town when you were busy making money for yourselves from their share.

The villagers doped with hope failed to realize the reality and fell prey to your plot. You tricked them to believe in your falsehood.

The village folk trusted you and fell for the funds allotted to them. They never suspected you and kept dreaming. Your life thrived and the poor villager's dream died.

Knowledge's stream meanders, in brains educated

I share not your loot in education you traded

Cash flowed from coffers, for pupils to read books

Books rested in cash books, cash nourished the crooks;

They came in droves to learn, no book or the boot

Lesson taught you learned ones, education alias loot;

A thousand teachers paid, not one came to teach

Money at a hand's distance, education out of reach;

Glow of wealth blinded, wisdom's eye for learning

Lit dark alleys of education, a hundred hearts burning."

The urban educated have all the knowledge to earn money, even by duping the simple rural folk. I do not share your spoils in the looting of the uneducated.

Funds for the purchase of books remained in the books. The books never reached the readers, but the cash reached the swindlers.

Seekers of knowledge came in large numbers. They were not provided the means to learn. The lesson they learnt from you was that education was a systematic loot of public funds.

Teachers were employed to teach but few actually came to the classrooms. Exchange of money prevented exchange of knowledge.

The educated got blinded by the glitter of money. The seat of learning was well lit, but the pupils remained in the darkness of ignorance.

CHAPTER 35

THE BETTER YOU – A CAUTION FROM ETHER AND EARTH

"Dug deep wormholes, into nature's rich mines

I share not your loot from betrayal of science;

Many came running, for a glimpse of modern knowhow

Deceived by the facade, the naive didn't know how;

Wizards of digital wisdom, ensured millions obsessed

In bits and bytes vanished, wealth tangible possessed;

Cure for all maladies, science the magic wand

Priced for every potion, princely in tragic land;

In flashes you commune, in moments you receive

Riches on inventions, to enlighten or to deceive;

The scientific progress enabled you to plunder the natural resources with ease. I do not share your spoils in the loot of the Earth's riches.

People at large believed in the power of science and expected their life to improve. They watched in awe, but the benefits reached you.

The digital revolution brought fresh hope of justice and transparency. People did not realize that they were being looted silently on every tap of a button.

Science promised to provide facilities to improve the living standard of the masses. You priced them so high that only the rich could afford and the poor kept suffering.

Dealings became easy for people like you, thanks to the technology. You had a new and more effective device to loot or to educate people.

Injected doses toxic, on Mother Nature's ailments

I share not your loot on scarce Earthly elements;

Earning heftily, you left, your breath to pollute

Mindless of the hurt, every rule you dilute;

Littered without a thought, the scavengers held sway

Street turned to sewage, you looked the other way;

Mouths multiply ever, to grow they eat and drink

Rampant growth concrete, lakes and rivers shrink;

Wormholes drilled in Earth, to scoop up ores

Your pet untamed, the beast of pollution roars."

You added more poison to the already polluted world. I do not share your exploits in illegal trade of natural resources.

Unaware of the dangers and the implications of reckless mining, you flouted all rules to make a fortune for yourself.

When the environs were being polluted and streets left for scavengers to roam, you took no action to cleanse them.

The ever increasing population demands food and water. The need for shelter turned green jungles into concrete. The life sustaining water bodies made way for the dead concrete structures.

With more excavation and mining of ores for human consumption, the threat of pollution multiplies.

CHAPTER 36

THE BETTER YOU – A CAUTION ON POWER AND ENERGY

"Bands in group dacoity, display fine synergy

I share not your loot in divested power, energy;

Energy drained to last ounce, of hapless, feeble, needy

To power your family, of ever hungry greedy;

Makers of your dreamland, never set the sun

Daughter shines all day, in night shines the son;

Lit up your home, the life's light you stole

Cursed brethren deprived, on thorny beds roll;

For body soul's union, seeker's body burns

Stealing their fuel, wheel of fortune turns;

You and your likes formed gangs to deprive and drain the people of the power and energy so much necessary to light up their homes. I do not share your exploits in the theft in the energy sector.

You channeled the energy meant for the people to power your home. Your greedy family never questioned your means of earning and enjoyed the luxuries.

Those of you who planned to loot people never faced difficult times. Your relative thrived on the wealth you earned through illegal means.

People were deprived of their basic needs and they led a poor life. They suffered daily but you and your family rolled in comfort.

People bore hardship for survival. Every day was a battle to keep body and soul together. You cheated them and made a fortune for yourself.

Gained strength in number, poachers get bold

I share not your loot in ravished green gold;

Jewels of forest felled, nature's beauty torched

Planted jungle concrete, troops civilized marched;

Cleared hurdles in progress, stately trees with saw

Humans claimed the forest, the beast mutely saw;

You severed the limbs and lungs, a silent vivisection

Tailored nature in town, a perfect self-deception;

That shook hands with skies, nurtured for decades

In moments fell to ground, bless the saws and spades."

The number of people like you, who joined the band of dacoits swelled and emboldened them. I do not share your spoils in the plunder of the natural wealth.

Trees were felled and land denuded to make way for the human settlement. Civilizations rose up in concrete to replace the floral civilization.

You uprooted and cleared all that came in way of progress. The beast in humans occupied the forests and the wild beast was rendered homeless.

The trees that formed the vital organs for the survival of the ecosystem got cut as humans tailored nature to suit their needs, hoping to ensure a better future.

Nature took ages to grow and preserve the forests and embrace all the creatures. The human hands raged the tall trees to the ground in no time.

CHAPTER 37

THE BETTER YOU – A CAUTION ON RIGHT CHEMISTRY

"Few gritty breathe freely, in hostile surrounding

I share not your loot in unethical chemical bonding;

Sap of life you rationed, strength benign diluted

Starved nature's children, left to die or looted;

Where tender balm demanded, you gave them pain

Insult rubbed on wounds, dipped in caustic rain;

Wanton wants bellowed smoke, shrunk guts and lungs

Choked Samaritan's throat, you waggled your tongues;

Mother Nature's recipe, brewed out of proportion

Profit your only goal, snatched away life's portion;

People with all comforts survive in hostile environs. Those who are naturally strong can face the adverse conditions created by human beings by polluting the ecosystem. I do not share your spoils in the poisoning of the habitat.

You and your gang deprived others of their share. You contaminated every element and fed it to the poor and weak who thus became susceptible to exploitation.

You never cared for the sick but wounded them more by abusing and depriving them of the basic necessities, instead of tending to their wounds.

Your greed and selfish demands snatched the rightful share of the weak and thus starved them. They wreathed in pain but your satiated being danced with joy.

Mother Nature provides balanced and wholesome means to all the creatures for a healthy living. You disturbed the delicate balance of nature for your gains and poisoned the lives of others.

With no heart to care, nor willing mind to force

I share not your loot in wasted human resource;

Masses flock for humane hand, holding for support

That came to be obliged, they oblige, you deport;

They labour even in pain, for you labour a pain

A pin pricks your heart, like mother's labour pain;

On months of gestation, a marvel of nature produced

It wanders in your den, to a commodity you reduce;

No value for Adam, nor care for human resource

Item of your consumption, Eve a perennial source."

There is none amongst you to care for the humanity or make the ones responsible to discharge their duty. I do not share your spoils in the exploitation of fellow citizens.

People expect the authorities to fulfill their needs and support them when in trouble. They rightly deserve to be served but you make them serve you.

The poor citizens work hard even if their bodies cannot take the load. For you even working hard is also a painful affair. They endure great pain due to your apathy and for you even the prick of a pin seems a deathblow.

A child is born after the mother endures excruciating pain. The precious gift of nature is left to your mercy to be reduced to an item of utility.

You have no empathy for your own fellow beings. You consider men and women to be inexhaustible source of slaves.

CHAPTER 38

THE BETTER YOU – A CAUTION ON RIGHT LIVELIHOOD

"Dragged your feet to give, but sprinted for receiving

I share not your loot in the battle to earn a living;

Tied in cuffs of bribe, hands that turned the wheel

One bowed to you smiled, rest left to sigh and squeal;

Seekers of livelihood sincere, the sole bread earner

Lost, wonder in your maze, a trap that bred you, sinner;

You gagged them to silence, the deserved but uncared

Heaped upon you curses, wished to avenge but scared;

Your greed blessed the donors, the haves got it easy

Rocking cradle of hope, the have-not kept busy;

You hesitated to help others but were ever eager to receive gifts from those who needed help. I do not share your spoils in the exploitation of the Ernest workers.

Those who were deserving and willing were denied employment by you for not greasing your palms. You honoured the undeserving as they were willing to bribe you.

The sincere ones ran from pillar to post to secure a job. They kept trying but failed as you set hurdles and traps for all seekers of job.

The helpless ones could not counter you as they were afraid. You never let them voice their protest against you.

The ones who donated generously were rewarded by you with good jobs. The honest ones without money were left out to struggle for livelihood.

The road taken once, never wished for reincarnation

I share not your loot on rogue's road to destination;

Uneasy lies the traveler, on road rail or in air

Down the docks went bribe, shipped to your lair;

Called for a moment's attention, cried every station

Wealth's wagon rolled in time, you timed devastation;

Cleared all kinks and blocks, for your stock arrived

Held to wait forever, the poor traveler cried;

All eyes on sacred baggage, the loot reached safe

You left passengers hapless, tricked, tired all but safe."

The traveler once takes to the road, never thinks of taking a second ride. I do not share your spoils in the laying of roads to doom.

Money spent to construct the various modes of transportation brought no comfort to the traveler. The bribe traveled the right path to your den.

The facilities you promised to create by spending huge amount never got the attention and care you promised. You promptly made payments ensuring a hefty share for yourself.

You cleverly cleared all the hurdles in your path to profit and never bothered for the poor travelers who waited patiently for their rightful share of comfort.

You took care to ensure that the loot of public money reached safely to the dishonest people like you. Others were left languishing, neither cared nor safe.

CHAPTER 39

THE BETTER YOU – A CAUTION ON JUDICIOUS FISCAL PLANNING

"With mind boggling proportions the mind reels

I share not your loot in shady financial deals;

By planner's magic wand, in air bridges float

Your spell holds the bridges, for riches to bloat;

Deserts in planning charts, with aqua pure you flood

Dripping sweat in the Sun, the labour draws blood;

Soft pulp of your accounts, hungry borers drill

They make millions, the labour an easy kill;

Some invested in honesty, you drove them out of business

You cheated them in millions, honest lacked your prowess;

The mammoth scale of financial scams numbs the brain of the common people. I do not share your spoils in the unethical financial dealings.

Bridges and roads are planned with grand designs and money is paid for the works. They exist only on paper, but the money enriches the ones with the evil design.

You promise people the unthinkable, unrealistic facilities. The poor labour works hard and sheds blood to realize the dream project.

You work hard on paper to nibble the public wealth. You get rich quickly, but the industrious lot does not get their share.

A few honest businessmen do try to work for the benefit of the people but are discouraged and forced to give up by you. You cheat people in millions and have no opposition as the common people have no power or craftiness like you.

Wage a war unethical, when losing call armistice
I share not your loot in maiming law and justice;

Justice for voice unheard, by lords, laws framed
By unjust hearing impaired, many a gullible framed;

Bartered time with law, justice delivered late
Law dragged the hearing, till victims prefixed late;

Law's courtship with outlaws, banished fear of law
Honest lawyer's advice, steer clear of law;

Neutral judge or advocate, a species hard to locate
For pleader of justice, legal course not advocate."

You care not for law and justice when waging a war against honesty. As long as you profit, you fight, but when at loss, you call a truce. I do not share your spoils in the fight against truth.

Laws are framed by the lawful to ensure justice for the weak. The law deafened by the jingle of coins does not hear the plea of the poor who suffer or are held guilty.

Justice delayed is justice denied. By the time decision is taken by the court, which postpones judgment and adds never ending hearings, the honest suffer irreparable losses.

The unethical relation between the guardians of justice and the criminals has no deterrence effect on the criminals. Some honest practitioners of law advise people to settle matter out of court.

Legal experts who are unbiased and who believe in dispensing justice to the weak are difficult to find. Those who need justice are advised not to approach the court for justice.

CHAPTER 40

THE BETTER YOU – A CAUTION ON SELF IDENTITY

"Sores on alien wings, the valued vulture

I share not your loot in erosion of culture;

A guide to misguide the youth, alien values slapped

Naive converts of pied culture, in piper's glory clapped;

At hefty costs you ushered, trends grand, exotic

Victims patrons, poor, rich, scholar or lunatic;

On wings glided glamour, flew out wisdom, wealth

Culture's vulture unwelcome, crash landed with stealth;

Generations on end, steeped in culture modern

Lost identity but your goal, by any mode to earn;

Patrons of foreign culture think they are elite and superior to the masses. I do not share your spoils in the degradation of the native culture.

You copy the ways of the foreigners and try to impose them on your people. You misguide the youth and glorify the alien culture.

You import items, ideas and ideals paying hefty price and victimize the naïve, financially poor, culturally bankrupt, and neo-intellects.

Glamour and vanity arrived to drive out wisdom and robbed the people of their wealth. The alien culture invaded undetected and unsuspected.

Generations lost touch with their native culture. You introduced them to modern culture and robbed them of their identity and grew rich on their wealth.

Sports or a battle, players at daggers drawn

I share not your loot in war of brain and brawn;

Labour hard for honour, get meager for their toils

Watch the dual unfold, bystanders collect the spoils;

For name and fame of nation, swallow dust and dirt

They tend to cuts and blisters, as you roll in comfort;

Humble proud gladiator's, esteem crashed to ground

For fighting they get penny, for facade you get pound;

Sportive as their spirit, they fought for every medal

Your nature a spoilsport, in every game you meddle."

In any kind of tussle, be it war or sports, the contenders pour their life to excel. I do not share your spoils in your game of deceit.

The players engage in the contest with total commitment. They stake all their energy and skills to win and bring honour to their nation. They are rewarded less for their hard work but spectators like you make a fortune.

The players get injured and still tend to their wounds to play for another day displaying indomitable spirit. They suffer in silence, but you need all comforts to witness their suffering.

The spirited players are hurt physically as well as psychologically when they watch you enjoy their agony and you are rewarded for your indifference and insensitivity.

They continued to toil and improve their skills as that is their nature. Your nature is to interfere in their field without having any knowledge of the sports activities and spoil their performance.

CHAPTER 41

THE BETTER YOU – A CAUTION ON SELF EXPRESSION

Art of expression faded, in the art of dilution

I share not your loot in the art of collusion;

Your art is in concealing art, what pays you promote

One applauded as artist, that your glory wrote;

Genius no guarantee, to adorn fame's jacket

Made business of art, genius warmed your pocket;

Devoid of vision just, you saw diamonds as stones

Into the fire of ignorance, many a classic thrown;

Devoted to art divine, kings of art chase ghosts

Devoted to wealth and wine, alien to art raise toast;

You lowered the quality of art by colluding with the traders of art. I do not share your spoils in the dilution of art.

You hide the artist and the art that is not profitable to you. You promoted those who glorified you and danced to your tunes.

With you as a judge, skill and hard work does not guarantee fame and recognition. The art that made you rich and that promotes your business gets promoted.

You could never see art beyond your business. You never valued true artists who lost their share due to the ignorance of their patron.

The true geniuses languished due to lack of judges who could recognize their talent. People like you who have no taste or wisdom to honour real talent profit from the art that is alien to them.

Devil's mind works overtime, for a new idea

I share not your loot with scary social media;

Movie, media, magic, welcome in grand reception

Casting hypnotic spell, masters of mass deception;

Your jaundiced vision spell doom, for some fate sealed

Robbers rejoice freely, your deeds kept truth concealed;

Lies lie above the truth, hidden behind the glamour

Should gossip summon guile, to tell truth from rumour;

Scandals, scams aplenty, how and why all wondered

You liberally honoured one, that was socially slandered."

The ones that think evil work overtime to deceive people and profit from the misfortune of others. I do not share your spoils in the misrepresentation by media.

All performing arts like movies, magic, and the media welcome people to their folds. They need publicity to sustain themselves for which they systematically deceive people in believing things that they show or voice.

You use the audio-visual instruments to hide the truth and show what you see as truth. Your acts put people to loss and the criminals rejoice in the freedom they enjoy in twisting the truth.

Lies are aired freely to hide the truth. The glitter and glow of untruth overshadows the truth. The gossip told repeatedly becomes truth and none dares to tell the truth from the lies.

The media showcases the scandals and scams glorifying them indirectly. You respect and fear those who are evil and praise those who are not revered by the people.

CHAPTER 42

THE DEVOTEE'S COMPULSIONS

Said the Devotee:

"I thank you for your wisdom, you read my mind

Revelations so vivid, nowhere else could I find;

Your words sooth my soul, and dampen my revulsion

Vision rid of clutter, to watch with care my compulsion;

I am made to pay, when I encounter my tribe

None wants to relent, without a share of bribe;

Refuse to team up, and I face social seclusion

Turn into a black sheep, feel safe in collusion;

In colony of robbers, the honest one gets a boot

Nowhere to go, I subscribe to the collective loot;

The Devotee said:

You have described the mindset and the thinking of the common people and have cleared my doubts. I am thankful to you for the words of wisdom.

My mind is at peace on seeing the true picture of the society. I can see my compulsions and limitations more clearly now.

My own clan forces me to pay bribe for getting things done. They too are in the same situation but no one wants to display honesty.

When I revolt and try to be honest, I find myself being ostracized. I am accepted and respected when I too join them and then I feel safe in their company.

One who is honest and fair is not accepted in the gang of robbers. Unable to fight the system, I too unwillingly join them in the collective loot of the national wealth.

Those blind to justice, on them never stares penury

My body's wounds pain, more the soul's injury;

Dare practice not, what I and the preachers preach

Who ensures to home, honesty would safely reach;

A few hands that clean, soon tire cleaning the muck

Filthy minds sleep well, the tired hands empty stomach;

A group of stooges, no strings bound to courage

Minds tied to slavery, mouth not limbs for outrage;

Your clan lords over, a school of submissive fools

We shall turn the wheels, you shall set the rules."

Those dishonest beings who care not for law and justice enjoy all the benefits and are never seen deprived. I bear physical and mental torture seeing the plight of people like me.

I would never try to practice what I preach or the good Samaritans advocate. People who want to practice honesty are never safe in a corrupt society.

Those gritty ones who try to clean the society tire themselves fighting the evil. They sleep without food whereas the corrupt sleep peacefully.

Some people criticize corruption and the corrupt but lack courage to take any action against them. They meekly continue serving the criminals like slaves.

Leaders rule the masses who have lost their will to fight for justice. The leaders dictate them and they labour helplessly for the lords.

CHAPTER 43

THE DEVOTED'S COMPULSIONS

Said the Devoted:

"So many of my clan, would reach the stately seat

Your compulsions to fret, their compulsion to cheat;

You take promises, that you let me not keep

Just your demands, and in peace I shall sleep;

When some demand honesty, and not rock the boat

No options when corporates, breathe down my throat;

With show of strength, make the outer worlds revere

High and mighty leader, haunts the underworld's fear;

Our loyal bonds snap, under the wealthy weight

Love for wealth turns, healthy love to hate;

The Devoted said:

Leaders make it to the seat of power with their compulsions. People feel helpless and can only vent their frustration and anger against the leaders. The leaders have to resort to malpractice to get power.

People place unjust demands to be fulfilled honestly by their chosen leader. They expect the leader to be honest and also oblige them for the vote they cast. If the voter has just demand, the leader won't have difficulty in meeting them.

Some people display honesty and let the leader play a fair game. The world of business demands that I betray the people and grant them their wish and they promise high rewards for the favour.

The leader is respected and feared by people due to the power the leader wields. The same leader fears the outlaws that rule the underworld.

The promise of loyalty and honesty is not honoured by the voter and the leader due to their individual compulsions. The love for wealth sows the seeds of hatred between the two.

You oblige the one, a leader's garb that dons

Noble ones hard to come, chosen ones–cons;

Wheel of progress profane, run by men in business

If not obliged amply, my fate you may well guess;

A cohesive force civil, team of servants humble

Serve them not, even the mighty leaders tumble;

Many strings attached, to the preachers of god

One unpleasant tug, the divine calls me fraud;

Forces umpteen thaw me, their vote–a favour granted

Wishes unethical yours, but honest leaders you wanted."

You elect the one you feel will lead you. You do not find fair and honest leaders. The chosen one poses as an honest leader but turns out to be a fraud.

The world runs on the policy of give and take. The people in business call the shots as they have wealth. If the leader refuses to oblige them they would not fund the leader and the party.

The administration of a nation or a state is managed by the civil servants. They draft rules and regulations. If they are not favoured, they would hamper smooth functioning of the government.

The religious community plays a major role in the election process. They polarize people to vote a particular leader. If the leader does not meet their demands, they would call a fraud.

You, the voters, make all these unethical and corrupt factions, who blackmail me for the vote you cast. The corrupt expect a leadership that is fair to them and at the same time, honest to the society.

CHAPTER 44

THE UTOPIAN RULE

Said the Devotee:

"You are the custodian, of justice and power

On your command peace and happiness shall shower;

Wealth of nation, for each one in abundance

Provide for all and display your providence;

Food for all mouths, with stocks full in harvest

Spare for rainy day, fill stomachs with the rest;

Enough bricks and blocks, for each head a roof

Grand stalls of luxury, riches need no proof;

Yarn spun in tons, spin around the shivering

Rags priceless in fashion, lot saved for covering;

The Devotee said:

You, the political leaders, have all the power and resources to meet the requirement of the people. You should provide for the people who elected you to power and oblige.

Each nation has plenty of wealth to look after the needs of the people. The same needs to be used judiciously to benefit the masses.

The nation produces enough food to feed the people. Even after saving emergency supplies there remains abundant food to feed the hungry.

Each individual needs shelter to live peacefully. There is enough material to build houses for all. Palaces and grand marvels of architecture are a testimony to the riches of a nation.

The nation produces clothes in tons that can be made available to the ones who shiver in the cold. The fashionable rags have become priceless and can save enough yarn for the needy.

Learning lent to each, powered to banish ignorance

Knowledge–the elixir of life, through each vein runs;

Collage of skills to display, none to be deprived

Work for a healthy living, for each one that arrived;

Health for the unfortunate, the prey of misfortune

Shred fat bills for pills, care on time opportune;

Wealth stacked uncounted, some grope in debt

Equal share for all, ensure penury no one met;

With promises for masses, rules the creature wisest

Food or fodder with a smile, shall the Devoted digest."

Every citizen needs education to lead a respectable life and to earn livelihood. Knowledge empowers one to progress.

Each one must get an opportunity to showcase one's skill. The abundance of talent available with each individual should be duly recognized.

The unlucky who fall prey to diseases need to be treated and cured. The costly treatment and medication must not deprive them of timely care.

The sharing of wealth is highly prejudiced, with the favoured ones getting richer and the neglected ones living in poverty. You can distribute wealth equally so that no one is poor.

You, the wisest of all the citizens, promise the citizens a happy and content life. Even you would not be comfortable leading a life full of uncertainties.

CHAPTER 45

THE RULE OF INEQUALITY

Replied the Devoted:

"Movement–the sign of life, the impulse of creation

Devotee, know the static, being Creator's negation;

Matter and mind travel, far and wide in disorder

One's being sees the truth, in one's vision broader;

Nay to heart of universe, to throb in equilibrium

No life propels to diversity, sans Nature's delirium;

Clouds of droplets form streams, rivers join the ocean

Driven by Sun the energy globe, set in eternal motion;

Matter cooks and freezes, in winds hot and cold

Spews elements varied, lowly dust, precious gold;

The Devoted said:

Creation needs a force to push matter and disturb the inertia. Absence of movement indicates the absence of the creator.

One's thoughts and the matter that one perceives, gain mobility only when the inertia is overcome. One realizes this fact when one sees beyond the mundane events of life.

The world would not have taken shape in the absence of an unbalanced driving force. The variety of life forms that emerged on the planet would not have been possible without nature prodding the elements.

The formation of clouds, rivers and oceans has its impulse in the celestial Sun. The Sun ensures that self and all entities around it are in perpetual motion.

One finds matter in different states due to the variation in temperature. The forces of nature transform matter into varied forms. The human being finds some priceless and some valueless.

Nature's web of survival, torments predator and prey

Paints creatures in shades, colour-blind sees all grey;

Armed with weapons, some dawn a garb ferocious

Hapless, meek lambs, some pray to god gracious;

None would perish if, all skills equally match

If limbs forget to spring, claws forget to scratch;

Without pressure supreme, diamond remains coke

Flora's heart would dry, fauna's lungs would choke;

The game of evolution, ensures the boon of quality

Cruel it may seem, none skirts the rule of inequality."

Nature ensures that each creature struggles to keep alive and propagate its kind. In a world of tough competition survival is not easy. This struggle gives rise to a variety of species with different survival skills.

Some creatures evolved as predators, armed with jaws and claws. Some are weak and humble with skills to escape the predators.

If the organism does not evolve and develop survival skills to outsmart the enemy, it would be killed. Such variety in flora and fauna would not be possible if all species had the same traits.

Just as carbon needs tremendous pressure to turn into a diamond, creatures need pressure to survive and improve their skills. In the absence of the stimulus, the plant and animal life would perish.

The spirit to live and fight the forces of nature and the natural enemies strengthens the species. The nature's balance sometimes seems cruel and favouring the powerful ones, but it is this inequality that drives the world and keeps it improving.

CHAPTER 46

POLITICS ILL DEFINED

Said the Devoted:

"One that gets power, inherits the secret vault of tricks

Shunned by moral judges, mobbed by loser eccentrics;

One robbed the masses, other set out to scavenge

Judge called a scam, the robber politics of revenge;

One steered projects mammoth, other stalled conception

Law called a racket, the racketeer politics of deception;

One built roads on maps, other called an inquiry

Court called laundering, the builder politics of treachery;

One performed shows of grandeur, other torched the stage

Code called cleansing of evil, the actor politics of rampage;

The Devoted said:

One who is elected to power knows the crafty ways of governance. The morally upright and law abiding ones avoid getting into Politics but the ambitious and power hungry losers pester the victor for justice.

The ruling party deprives the people and amasses wealth. The opposition party sees an opportunity to demand its share and calls it a lawful exposure of scam. The rulers see it as an act of revenge.

The rulers make grand plans and ambitious projects. The opposition prevents them from implementing them and calls it a lawful exposure of a racket. The rulers see it as act to deceive and misguide the people.

The rulers plan roads that may never be built. The opposition calls for an inquiry and calls it a lawful exposure of money laundering. The rulers see it as an act of treachery against the welfare of the people.

The rulers put up shows highlighting the achievements of the party. The opposition attacks the facade and calls it lawful destruction of the evil. The rulers see it as an act of hooliganism.

One claimed tall achievements, other proved propriety
Verdict called plagiarism, claimant–politics of dacoity;

One let loose the accused, other called for reason
Bench called collusion, the con politics of treason;

One welcomed unethical dealings, other blocked the trade
Rule called swindling, the swindler politics of hatred;

One destroyed records, the other appeared with data
Magistrate called betrayal, culprit personal vendetta

People worshiped one or the other, both stripped off secrecy
The voted called bitter truth, the voter–politics of plutocracy."

The rulers take credit for all the progress but the opposition claims to pioneer the process towards progress. One accuses the other for resorting to plagiarism.

The rulers absolve the suspects accused of committing crime by the opposition. The other party raises an objection against the verdict but the benefactor calls it a plot.

The rulers resort to unlawful means in business and the opposition tries to stall the deal calling it plunder of public money. The rulers call it a game of hatred and jealousy.

The rulers erase records of crime committed by them. The opposition brings more evidence against the rulers and accuses them of breaching the trust of the people. The rulers call it an act of revenge.

The masses elect the leaders who, they think, are honest. The leaders are exposed by their own clan. The politicians call it the reality of politics. The voter sees it as a rule of the rich and the powerful.

CHAPTER 47

POLITICS WELL DEFINED

Said the Devoted:

"When, with past, the present generations compare

Together, parent and child call politics of welfare;

Less starve for nourishment, for every ailing treatment

Gaining strength, young and old call politics of betterment;

Facade cared not, claps for face ugly or pretty

Skill sole measure, peers and public call politics of austerity;

Laid to rest differences, all creeds find fusion

Faith ignites, blind and seers call politics of vision;

Burden the masses not, with poor or rich the corpus

Calm, content, poor and rich call politics of purpose;

The Devoted said:

While comparing the rule of the yester years with the present, the guardians and the wards should call it good governance for the welfare of the people.

Less people found to be deprived of food and medical treatment. The week ones gain strength. The young and the old call it a governance for the betterment of the masses.

Not falling for the outward appearance and show, the viewers clap for the performance and skill of the artists. The artists and the masses call it governance of non-indulgence.

All races, castes and groups sink their differences and come together to form a united human race. The non-enlightened and the visionaries call it a governance of vision.

The nation may not be rich but it does not extract wealth unreasonably from the masses. The subjects are satisfied with whatever they have. The rich and the poor call it governance with a purpose to keep the people happy.

Collage ethnic and exotic, of cultural exuberance

Enthralled, critic and creators call politics of tolerance;

Gift of true democracy, varied rulers rule in sequels

Empowered, voter and voted call politics of equals;

Faithful souls provide ground, for honesty to practice

Blindfold visionaries and petitioners call politics of justice;

Summon all brave, to banish fear of gender or age

Mind body safe, mighty and weak call politics of courage;

Devotee and Devoted, scribe to script tale of remembrance

Heretics and historians, call politics alias good governance."

The nation has a canvas painted with the cultures of various races. The ones who created the collage and the ones viewing it appreciate it with tolerance from a different perspective. The critics and the creators call it governance of liberal and accommodative minds.

In a democracy, rulers come and go. They rule one after another and carry on the good work with equal opportunities for all. The voter and the leader call it governance of equal rights and duties.

In a land where honest people provide a stage for the fair and just people to perform their duties, even the blindfolded legal system and the seeker of justice call it a just governance.

Encouraging the brave and the bold to undertake difficult tasks without fear and promising them adequate safety and insurance is the task of the rulers. The weak and the powerful ones call it governance of the gallantry.

Where the voter and the voted work together to write a tale of just and healthy politics, the orthodox and the devoted define politics as good governance.

CHAPTER 48

THE VERSES OF CAUTION

Said the Devoted to Devotee:

"Works and verses literary, spiritual way of life preaches

Body worshiped, adored, yet spirit to no one reaches;

Virtues vain and vanity, are seldom put to test

Outward pomp venerated, soul is put to rest;

Few erudite trace tradition, to claim lofty idea

Neo-erudite a race, that races to hug the media;

Values that made races known, people cherished

People made races unknown, thus values perished;

Fruits of wisdom, never plucked from holy psalms

Soft and smooth gems of wisdom, slip off greasy palms;

The Devoted tells the Devotee:

All great works and writings preach to lead a pious and moral life. The works are praised and are worshiped, but the teachings are forgotten.

Social and spiritual values are not tested and adopted in life. However, the facade and the display of vanity are greedily embraced leaving the values.

The thinking, intellectual class connect all their lofty ideas to a great tradition of their race. The new initiates are in a hurry to air their opinion through the ever receptive media.

Ideas and ideals that identified with great races and intellectual giants were venerated by all. The new breed of thinkers slighted them and hence values got diluted.

Words of wisdom, great works and things of social value found no takers. These gems slipped through the hands that were busy collecting vile wealth.

Flattery, words of honeyed tongue, drug for sedation

Sweet dreaming sleepwalkers, worthy of predation;

Poured out thanks in millions, with whom voters trade

Dared not those who lost, call a spade a spade;

One that gained and that lost, both kept truths concealed

Dreams of millions untrue, in ballot boxes sealed;

Hands made ready for ballot battles, few verses they wrote

Read the minds that read your mind, before casting vote

Clever voters do favour none, doubt leader's dry verse

Voter, looter hand in glove, beware of Politics diverse."

People believed the sweet words and the false promises of the leaders. Though awake, they dreamt of a bright future and acted as if sedated and fell victim to the predators.

The voters thank the winners in anticipation that they will be helped in fair or foul weather. The losers know the truth about the unfair demands of the people but would not speak out.

The winners and the losers kept the secret of gaining votes and power from the people. The votes cast during the elections decide the fate of the people.

The leaders who fight elections and struggle for gaining power never educated the masses about unfair demands and gained votes. The voter should know that the leaders can read their mind when they cast their vote.

The voters who are aware of the ballot battles, should not believe false electoral promises and understand that the game of Politics, both fair and unfair, is played by the voter and the voted together. The fields of political battle are diverse in nature.

CHAPTER 49
POLITICS OF HUMAN DIVERSITY

"Living mosaic of beings, houses creatures of every kind
Kind to own kind, with others have an axe to grind;

Each life–fauna or flora, varied robes they wore
Each one a foe to tame, herbivore or carnivore;

Shrunk world's expanses, made own species a rival
Human poachers up in arms, in the struggle for survival;

Worlds uncivilized became, subjects of nature's diktat
Civilized humans tailored nature, benign scientific act;

Tenants of Terra-firma, dwarfs or giants of the race
Differ, with place terrestrial, in colour, form and face;

The Earth is a mosaic made up of a combination of all sorts of creatures. Each one tries to protect and propagate own species but is ready to pounce on others.

Plants and animals come in diverse forms. Each one has a natural enemy to deal with and protect itself. The harmless and timid herbivores and the ferocious carnivores, both face the same difficulties for survival and threat to their lives.

Human beings claimed the Earth as their own property and expanded territorial control by encroaching into others' land. Right to live transformed into a fight to survive in the human society itself.

The uncivilized animals followed the natural ways without disturbing the balance of nature. The civilized humans dictated nature and shaped it to suit their liking, using their mental faculty that helped them tame Nature.

The humans are temporary inhabitants of planet Earth. The developed races and the ones still rooted to Mother Earth differ in appearance, shape and size as dictated by the environment they live in.

Cloned models down to a cell, similar under the skin

Shape and colour prod the mind, for factions from within;

Blessed with a mystic mind, pure human attribute

For struggle of a million years, Mother Nature's tribute;

Minds at peace fall asunder, if ill falls a part

Mighty mind falls ill, and the world falls apart;

You pray races to race, and follow virtue's orders

Nature reigns to negate, a world without borders;

While in a family some say, nay to fruit some to meat

Human family racial, wishes Heaven and Earth to meet."

All human beings have the same structure, matter and consciousness under the skin. Yet they are divided on the basis of their colour, contours and stature.

Human beings alone have the faculty of reasoning and the intellect to introspect, gifts bestowed by Mother Nature for their long struggle in the process of evolution.

The mind cannot work peacefully and sanely if some part of the body is not fit. The human world behaves in an insane manner when the intelligent minds fall ill.

You hope that all races would follow the path of the virtuous ones and all would progress. Nature designs the world in such a manner that there is no equilibrium.

In the human family itself the parents and the siblings are not similar in their tastes and likings. Yet the divided human species wishes the inequality in the human society to vanish.

CHAPTER 50

POLITICS OF RELIGIOUS DIVERSITY

"Tussle of brain and brawn, in nature settles scores

Arms physical harm a few, weapon of belief in crores;

A rift benign terrestrial, runs across the neighbour's reign

Belief contrived celestial, unseen yet a blinding screen;

Tribes ancient honoured, intellect with super vision

The civilized spelt truth, the skewed upheld superstition;

A lighter burden of faith, the earthy tribal possessed

Weighed down by generations, those with belief obsessed;

One cherished rituals and rites, factual or symbolic

Others scorned the sacred sacrifice, as acts diabolic;

In the struggle for survival, creatures use their brain and the muscle power to overpower their natural adversary. The weapon of belief which is solely a human possession, harms not only the enemies but also own fellow beings.

Evolution has created a divide between creatures to ensure equal opportunities for all to survive. The humans created walls of beliefs and superstitions that have been a cause of a million deaths.

The ancient tribes upheld the wisdom of their elders on the basis of their experience. The modern civilization saw truth through the scientific and logical eye. The ones who deliberately distorted the facts used superstitions to control and rule people.

The uncivilized tribal created and possessed lesser sects to believe and follow and hence were less tortured. The faithfully wealthy modern society is burdened and fragmented with the weight of their beliefs.

Beliefs, rites, and rituals of one section of society are not acceptable to the others. Human beings do not come to terms with their own wisdom.

Fought each other for ages, due vanity and vengeance

Giant minds clashed, hailing religion's emergence;

All claimed the god of their making, a few liberals spurned

Agree with demigods, else, on stake the non-believer burned;

Ran through each belief, a cord of intolerance uniform

Some captured it in stone, some without human form;

From this world to the celestial one, went wild imaginations

Sprang ferocious beasts from humans, across all nations;

Belief—the mind created, a weapon of mass destruction

Divided each to kill, promised dead one's resurrection."

Different sects and faiths quarreled endlessly for supremacy and to annul other faiths as revenge. The victorious giants established their own following and thus emerged the ancient religious groups.

The groups that emerged claimed their god's propriety over others'. Some moderates and liberals refused to tow the popular line and they along with the non-believers were prosecuted.

All faiths displayed intolerance or disagreement with others. Some worshiped god in a tangible form and some in subtler forms or without any form.

The religious ones invented energies and entities out of their faith as they perceived their truth. Their hallucinations and visions gave birth to various deities with superhuman powers, thus dividing the human civilizations among themselves.

The humans believed their self-created celestial deities and worshiped them to protect their clan and destroy the heretic. Their belief became a magic wand to bring their faithful dead to life and a weapon to execute the living who refused to follow their faith.

CHAPTER 51

POLITICS OF ECONOMIC DIVERSITY

"All are born seekers and beggars, states Nature's law

Rob Nature of its wealth and grow, for sure human flaw;

A few minds ignited, discovered Nature's abundance

Nations caged the minds, forced human dependence;

Gain of human race, the bloom of ancient economics

Race for gains scripted, new rules in human genomics;

Exchange need for need, a humble way of barter

Trader caught the winds, sailed as business starter;

Need one knead the needy, and force unwelcome trade

Greed's plot on a nation's freedom, a slow and stealthy raid;

All living creatures have to depend on what Nature offers them. Their existence is dictated by their skills to seek and get their means of livelihood.

The ancient intellectual giants discovered the abundance of resources in nature and invented ways and means to get them. The crafty, greedy ones used the knowledge gained from the wise ones and started dictating terms to Mother Nature.

The exploitation of natural resources paved way to the emergence of ancient economic strategies. This race for trade supremacy transformed humans into an unnatural breed that tried to tailor Nature to their liking.

People exchanged goods available with them for those they could not be supplied by nature around them. The need for merchandise encouraged people to sail and establish overseas trade.

The need for exotic goods brought trouble to the needy and the ones deprived by nature. Those who had the Nature's blessings exploited the ones who were deprived of it.

Wants grew in volume, thus evolved complex commerce
An ocean of opportunities, for political differences to immerse;

Some set minds free, but held in shackles profane treasure
Some states locked the mind, gifted prisoner in full measure;

Some task to capacity, provide for the toilers' needs
Others provide for capacity, that the provider heeds;

Nations got polarized, under wealth poverty submerged
Material worlds flourished, in tandem third world emerged;

Global economics binds nations, in relations as a swivel
Business of politics harbours, many a **Necessary Evil**."

As peoples' necessities increased, they expanded their trade and thus commercial dealings crossed borders. Trade brought the peoples of the world closer, rewriting political ideologies.

Some states valued monetary treasure and gave freedom to their citizens. The others cherished the noble minds but controlled them by rewarding them.

Some states made the masses to deliver as per employer's capacity and rewarded them for their work. Others made them work to each one's capacity and provided for the individual's needs.

Nations got divided into likeminded groups and accumulated wealth. Poverty of the nations was hidden behind the decorated curtain. World got divided into rich and poor nations based on the wealth they amassed and vanity they flaunted.

International trade forged strange alliance revolving around mutual benefits. Politics, a service of good governance, became a business, brooding many evil traders who eventually became a **Necessary Evil** for the Politics as practiced.

CHAPTER 52

THE CROOKED NATURE DESIGNER

Said the Devotee:

"Preserve the mortal world, all scriptures do insist

Devils fondly pampered, wonder why they exist;"

Said the Devoted:

"Desired holy Nature, to plant in humans a devil

Or Earth would be Heaven, hail the **Necessary Evil**;

To quench human thirst insatiable, Nature's laws braved

Tread forbidden path, in humans evil got enslaved;

Humble creatures laboured, human dwellings reared

Beneath urban blue print, green forests disappeared;

Divine planner of food chain, saw benign Nature nurtures

Brandished steely chain saw, canine greedy poachers;

The Devotee said:

All holy scriptures urge us to be compassionate to fellow beings and nurture the benign nature. I wonder why we have entities who are designed to damage the delicate balance of nature and bring misery to human beings as well as other creatures.

The Devoted replied:

Nature has designed its creation in such a way that there remains a balance between the good and the evil. If all evil and threatening elements disappear, then the process of evolution would stop and Earth would become a Utopian Heaven, as described in the holy texts.

The ever increasing desire for more luxuries propelled humans to fight nature and find ways to live in comfort. In their attempt to be happy, they crossed the limits as the evil in them reared its head.

All animals on Earth made their dwellings with whatever nature provided to meet their needs without disturbing the balance. The human civilization expanded to meet the requirements of the people. The environment being the sole provider got ravaged by the greedy humans.

The creators of the worlds made arrangements to feed all creatures as per their taste and appetite. Human beings hunted and poached not for food and shelter alone, but for satiating their hunger for luxury and profane pleasures.

Hunger for wealth scooped, precious minerals to dine
The wealthy stuffed their guts, the hungry dug the mine;

Treasure claimed by heir illegal, the legal guardian snores
To replace ponds and springs, spring up wells and bores;

Foragers in blood and bones, ensure none left as wastage
Million mouths metallic, salvage the mountains of garbage;

Deluge of human desires, filled rivers with chemicals
Task beyond humans to cleanse, waiting for miracles;

With airs of human progress, bellows the chimney's air
Nature poacher—a necessary evil, bear with solemn prayer."

The rich minerals and precious stones hidden in the bosom of Mother Nature were dug out by the greedy humans. The labours who worked hard to unearth the wealth slept hungry whereas the smart ones pocketed all the wealth.

Illegal mining and plunder of natural wealth went unnoticed by the guardians of the national property. Ponds and springs were also not spared to mine for the riches. Natural streams and lakes gave way to artificial structures like wells and bore wells.

The natural scavengers designed by nature to maintain the critical balance of nature did their duty of fixing the leftovers. Humans created so much of garbage that their mammoth machines are unable to clear the piled up waste.

The chemicals that are pumped in the rivers are a symbol of human desire to exert their power over nature. Nature can cleanse the pollution that is created by itself but the pollution created by the human beings is going beyond the capacity of Nature or humans.

The smoke that rises from the factories which human beings erected speaks of the progress made by them. The evil of poaching and polluting is necessary to prevent the Earth from becoming Heaven.

CHAPTER 53

THE DISEASED CHEMIST

"Making space for new, the old creations perish

Change–the only constant, holy creators cherish;

Excuse to be reborn, for aging life to cease

As invite to the last guest, to life gifted disease;

Wisdom delayed final meet, for nature planted curbs

For every tortured step, sprang up benign herbs;

Vice among the wise, got nature's gifts patented

Rich's roughs smoothened, human intellect dented;

Traded with health priceless, hankered for copyright

Nature's message of co-existence, not copied right;

As creatures age and get old, they leave this planet, making space for the new arrivals. This change in the habitants of the planet is the only constant activity.

The death of an organism is an excuse for more births to keep the species going. Life is gifted with old age and disease for death to take away the last visitor to the planet.

Human wisdom tries to delay the final meeting with death by using the natural hurdles in the path of death. The suffering humans discovered antidotes in the form of medicinal herbs.

Nature had freely gifted medicines to all creatures to get cured, but the greedy ones exercised control over the knowledge of medicines for their own benefit by patenting them. The ones who could afford got cured of sickness, but the human mind got sick with selfishness.

They made profits trading with the health of other fellow humans by claiming patents and copyrights of the medical knowledge. Nature's message of healthy living was understood but that of peaceful co-existence was not.

Cure for sickly beings, doctor's business to teach

Interns learn business, put medicines out of reach;

A step ahead of the devil, the humans achieved a feat

Death's loyal agent born, medicines counterfeit;

Saved for precious lives, the lifesaving medicine

The rich cured in shade, the poor paid for the Sin;

Prescribe even poor, the expensive exotic brand

Generic ones not potent, costly medicines grand;

Many to inject venom, to siphon few would dare

Dope Druggist–a necessary evil, bear with solemn prayer."

Doctors are tasked to teach their understudies to understand the business of curing the patients. Unfortunately, they learn the business of making money by selling medicine meant for the needy.

The evil human mind became even more corrupt and started making fake medicines and made money, an act that produced a killing agent that put the devil to shame.

Lifesaving costly medicines reserved for the needy poor were made available only to the privileged ones who were cured in the comfort of their homes. The poor suffered for the deeds of the sinners.

The costly medicines sold by big companies were prescribed to the poor who could not afford them. The affordable generic brands were not preferred as they were not profitable.

The business minded in health care administered poison instead of antidote. Few people in the service of health care dare to be loyal to the profession. The evil of drugging the patient is necessary to prevent the Earth from becoming Heaven.

CHAPTER 54

THE UNEDUCATED EDUCATOR

"Well before birth, parents spotted wisdom teeth

For pupil yet to arrive, the school reserved a seat;

Dream of right education, drained pockets dry

Parents and wards, with knowledge's burden cry;

Efforts centered around, the ward's future–scary

Toiled day and night for future, present left weary;

Fleeced one and all, did victims utter a word

Academic warriors proved, pen mightier than sword;

Compete due numbers, they in droves are drawn

Learned erudite hunter, trapped the green horn;

The expectant parents decided the caliber and intellect of their child who is yet to be born. They reserve a seat for the child in a school which they believe would impart quality education to the child.

Parents spend huge amounts for the right education of their wards. The financial requirement for it drains them of their hard earned money.

Every parent tries to secure a safe and comfortable future for the child and works hard to that effect. The desire for a bright future makes the present gloomy.

Those in the business of education robbed the rich and the poor alike. Both victims did not protest against the loot. The robbers proved that it does not take weapons to intimidate people. Words that harm psychologically are more powerful that weapons that harm physically.

Limited seats and a large number of pupils to seek admission drives them into a mad competition. The learned businessmen trap the new generation of parents and the future generation of infants into their net of wisdom.

Glad a seat ensured, pray their ward studies

Trap set in place, the educators earn with ease;

Life's lesson in classroom, meant pious life one shrugs

Wisdom sought to wake one up, one wallows in drugs;

Truth never graces blackboard, safe career one picks

Principal against principle, taught the pupil politics;

The master delivers lecture, pupil at receiving end

The wise in the grip of vice, the option—break or bend;

Walking into a free world, or leading into a wolf's lair

Vice teacher—a necessary evil, bear with solemn prayer."

Once they earn a seat in the school, the parents are assured that their child would study well and learn the lessons of life. The educator is happy with the catch trapped in the net of wisdom.

Pupils thus admitted and initiated learn to avoid an ethical and disciplined life. Some are drugged with immorality while others with sedative drugs. The education meant to awaken their talents puts them into a slumber.

Classrooms do not educate the pupils to stand up to truth and follow a collision course with untruth. Instead, they are taught to choose a path of least resistance by their mentors and resort to unfair play.

The tutor, infected with vices, teaches unholy practices to the taught who has no choice but to relent. Both have to flow with the current of immorality.

Education designed to lead a successful life in a free world lands the student into the den of the learned educator. The evil of a Vice Educator is necessary to prevent the Earth from becoming Heaven.

CHAPTER 55

THE PURITAN ADULTERATOR

"Truth—the only commodity, unstained by thought pristine

Each item of human consumption, cries hoarse for hygiene;

Polluted feed of the faithful ones, with labour one digested

Victims of greed, the unsuspecting, all with drugs ingested;

With sagacious beings, purity thus humans consumed

With malicious ones, the pure halted, the base resumed;

Not easy to catch, the adulterator dons a mask

To de-weed the healthy crop, a scary, daunting task;

Unmindful of the harm, own profit their food for thought

Teamed up hoarders of grain, to feed venom they fought;

Of all the items within the grasp of human beings and beyond, truth is one item that escapes all adulterates. Rest all items of human consumption are contaminated for profit.

People are fed with food laced with poisonous drugs and mixed with adulterates by the manufacturers and suppliers. The poor consumers, risking their lives, have to consume the venom and digest it.

When business was carried with honesty, purity of items was assured by the vendors. As the greedy and dishonest took to business, purity gave way to the defiled.

It is difficult to trap the ones in the business of adulteration. They escape the law as they morph themselves cleverly. To tell the real from the adulterated is a very difficult task.

Those who trade in impurities care not for the harm they cause to the consumers. They vie with one another and fight for their right to feed poison to the people.

Served superior stuff to consume, for those pro-fit

Unfit for consumption, fed to the frail for profit;

Life at risk for both, for one gains are huge

Outlaws mortgage morals, in law they take refuge;

Doctor treats the patient, the diseased skilled to doctor

Wean health from the healthy, with disease they barter;

Adulterates–the bread and butter, some bread and butter sacrifice

The heartless dealt death blows, to purity's crumbling edifice;

Crop of grains or human brain, both caught in a toxic snare

Immature Adulterator–a necessary evil, bear with solemn prayer."

Those aware of the healthy and unhealthy, got served superior quality products. The ones who were ignorant of the harmful effects of the goods, received the inferior lot. Health is traded for profit.

Those receiving and the ones supplying are consumers. Both are equally exposed to the health hazards. Profits being the driving force they succumb to the temptation. Even the laws do not ensure health of the citizens.

The medical fraternity labours to treat the patients but the real diseased persons, the ones that adulterate, know how to escape unharmed. Thus they trade in disease and not in health.

Some poison the very bread and butter that gives life, whereas some sacrifice their bread and butter for the good of society. Unmindful of the harm, some speed up the process of poisoning.

Food for the body and the mind, both got caught in the poisonous noose of greed. The evil of an Immature Adulterator is necessary to prevent the Earth from becoming Heaven.

CHAPTER 56
THE EMPLOYMENT EXCHANGER

"Hunt with gathered knowledge, means of livelihood
Hunters without knowledge, in worthy's way they stood;

A breed of seekers sincere, burnt the midnight oil
Lost the race unaware, daughter and son of soil;

Buoyed with joy the educated, till wisdom spilled
Hirer ensured many lives, under bribe's burden killed;

In a class of class nepotism, toppers faced relegation
For favoured posts ensured, wisdom's bane–reservation;

Skeptics reserved doubt, would merit get its reward
Corrupt reserved a berth, assured the privileged ward;

The students work hard to get equipped for a decent employment. In their search for it, they confront ignorant employers who care not for their skills and are a hindrance in their pursuit for a decent job.

Some students are industrious and they labour to get selected but lose the race and are not even aware that they have been cheated.

They are overjoyed seeing their performance in their institutions and are elated on acquiring a prestigious degree. The devil of corruption and nepotism engulfs them when they step out of their home into an unjust world of opportunities.

In a world that acts on recommendations, even the best students are not hired and are relegated to inferior positions. Reservation, an act meant to eradicate inequality in the society, is misused to create a rift between the skilled and the exploited.

The learned people are doubtful about the appreciation and acknowledgement of learning to be the sole criteria in selection. The biased employers are happy to grant jobs to their favoured candidates.

Life's ruthless compulsions, coerced to run the race

In simmering desert of corruption, mirages they chased;

Some lucky unprivileged, climb to the top with hope

Labour no match for favour, they tumble down the slope;

Efforts in vain to award a scholar, an unemployed degree

Right to right educators, should vouch the scholar's pedigree;

The connected do not need, knowledge for salvation

Disconnect with nepotism, knowledgeable die of starvation;

In good stead lays the patronized, mason or a mayor

Eely employer–a necessary evil, bear with solemn prayer."

Struggle for survival pushes the individual to hunt for job. All that is learnt in the schools seem irrelevant when one confronts corruption as a road block to progress.

A few bright and lucky ones top the list of aspirants with a hope of getting a good job but are shocked to know that even they are not assured of worthy employment.

Hard work and mental labour of the intelligent ones go waste in earning a degree that remains unemployed. The elderly, wise and the learned ones need to ensure that justice is done to the brighter and deserving lot.

If one is connected to those who use unfair means to employ their preferred candidates, one need not be good at studies. One who knows not the tricks of getting a job is likely to lose and remain jobless.

Those who are protected and pampered by the corrupt and influential lot of the society lead a secured life. The evil of an Unfair Employer is necessary to prevent the Earth from becoming Heaven.

CHAPTER 57

THE ALERT DRUG PEDDLER

"The chaos and frustration, pray prod one to meditate

Endless battles in mind, easy way–a pill to sedate;

Maiden dose to steer the soul, and stimulate senses

Hesitant mind it compels, the mind of will it cleanses;

A hope to the initiate, to hear light and see sounds

Deprive them of the dose, unleash a million hounds;

Better early than never, the peers catch them young

Set to poison the new-born, humans with forked tongue;

Addict bound to drugs, left relatives to mourn

Once related to drugs, even trade with death of own;

In a life full of insecurities and strife, some take to meditation. Others find an easy way out by consuming drugs to de-stress themselves.

The initiate finds it relieving when introduced to drugs. It removes the stress but also robs one of one's will, forcing one to get addicted to it.

One gets hallucinations and a feeling of wellbeing as one experiences bliss. When the drug is not available, one gets mad with rage.

Those who are looking for victims to promote drugs prefer to catch them in their early stage of life when they lack wisdom to cope with the harsh realities of life. These venomous creatures would not hesitate to drug even the infants to make huge profits.

The relatives of the addicted ones suffer for their deeds. Those who are once addicted to drugs would not hesitate to kill their loved ones to get their daily dose of drug.

The will, assured will wander, in the maze once lost

Spell bound it sleepwalks, the journey at any cost;

One's momentary lapse, brought for life addiction

Once bitten not to shy, and fight with benediction;

The prize of conjugal bliss, without tying the knot

Drugs shoot the morals down, with a single shot;

Caution the naïve victims, angels cry hoarse

To arrest none dares, to patron pills are scores;

Attempt to awaken wisdom, erodes wisdom's layer

Drug Peddler—a necessary evil, bear with solemn prayer."

Once addicted to drugs, it takes over the will of the addict and ensures that the one thus addicted will be a slave to the drug and continues living a life of a living dead, no matter how much the losses.

In times of difficulty, one succumbs momentarily and becomes an addict for life. The hesitation vanishes and one accepts and surrenders one's wisdom without a fight.

The desire for pleasures without responsibilities or awareness of the consequences, thereafter, sacrifices the moral values to drugs with the first ever experience with drugs.

There is enough preaching against the ill effects of drugs but rarely are the manufacturers punished. Those who propagate the use of drugs are far more active and powerful than those opposing them.

Those who attempt to eradicate the menace of drugs get demoralized due to the ineffective laws. The evil of a Drug Peddler is necessary to prevent the Earth from becoming Heaven.

CHAPTER 58

THE SPORTING WARRIORS

"Souls ignited, bodies athletic, molded as of clay

Battles bigger than sports, a bigger game to play;

Beacon all to trial and test, choose few to compete

A berth in the team is victory, prize gold or peat;

Some bear the burden of trust, to ensure fair play

Unnoticed behind the curtain, mischief on display;

Sight goals beyond horizon, eyes focused to win

Look beyond appearances, dark or fair the skin;

Victors dealt with firm handshake, medals bought with sweat

Losers shook hands with money, to buy with no regret;

The sportsmen and women are trained and enthused with national spirit and sportsmanship. Their personality is molded to achieve higher goals but they end up fighting battles outside the sports arena for justice.

They are tried and tested to prove their capabilities so as to earn a place in the team. Irrespective of the performance of the team in the competitions, selection itself is a major victory and an achievement in itself.

Some selectors and athletes play a fair game and trust the selection process. However, there are others who play cheat behind the screen, unnoticed by the honest players.

Sportspersons are trained to perform beyond their limitations to ensure victory. Their skills are the sole factor to be considered, leaving personal prejudices aside.

The ones who work hard and win, face the world with pride and self-esteem. There are others who spend money to buy trophies and feign victory compromising their integrity.

Players team to increase scores, scores ready to coach

Few treads the fair path, many the wrong approach;

Sporting team the flag bearer, to hoist the national pride

A privilege some undeserving bought, justice on the slide;

Where talent let down hope, bailed out official favour

Favour let down the talented, leaving a bitter flavour;

Players without a patron, in trials face a battle

In war of men and mean, many a Gladiators rattle;

Trailing a talent's track, the skilled player runs in despair

Medal Merchant–a necessary evil, bear with solemn prayer."

In sports events players come together as a team to gain strength and find coaches ready to train them. Many of them find it easy to take to foul play to be victorious.

The honest players feel proud and privileged to represent their nation and fly their flag high. Some players buy the privilege as they find some selectors who are willing to trade with their integrity.

Those who lacked talent but were ambitious, approached their patrons for undue favours. In the bargain, some talented players lost their place in the team leaving them dejected.

Players who compete solely on skills and have no influence, have to struggle to get selected. In the unfair battle for selection, many talented players lose.

Gifted and talented players, hon their skills and chase their goal in desperation. They work extra hard to beat the unfair players. The evil of a Medal Merchant is necessary to prevent the Earth from becoming Heaven.

CHAPTER 59

THE DIGITAL HACKER

"Computers superhuman count, on human mind to compute

Mind other's affairs not own, mind and machine in dispute;

Humanoid born of dead matter, mimic humans one wonders

Master turns a techno-slave, thus human wisdom blunders;

Mountain load of ancient knowledge, now reduced to bits

Locked in artificial intelligence, in bits and bytes that sits;

Riding crests and troughs, knowledge soars at speed of light

Digital progress of nimble digits, a journey from waddle to flight;

Hackers hide in thousands, infest the digital harvest

Malware this if unaware of, retards the brain's quest;

The fastest computer designed by humans depends on the inputs given by them to work. When both are in disagreement, there is sure to be a dispute.

Robots looking like human beings do just what humans do, and better. It is a wonderful machine created by them. Overdependence on the machines turns the master into a slave.

Knowledge of the past centuries saved in perishable scriptures and bulky documents is now saved in small gadgets. The exhaustive information is trapped in digital bits and bytes.

Exchange of information and transfer of sacred knowledge is possible in a moment over long distances. The creeping instrument of wisdom takes to flight.

There arrives an entity that intends to retard the progress of human beings and profit from it. The unethical hackers hidden in the digital society are the real threat.

Dots on a digital canvas, visual treat to mesmerize

Tasked for multiple tasks, limbs shrink to nano size

One that dons the white hat, the force multiplier

Steals for a cause patriotic, welcome the truthful liar;

Courtesy, the black hat hacker, tuskers dance to a tap

A wicked mind at work, draws high and mighty in trap;

By magic wand of programming, net mysteries deepen

In hands of benign hacker, the net a handy weapon;

Both faces of the coin, values the sovereign chair

Digital Hacker—a necessary evil, bear with solemn prayer."

The tiny dots on the display come together to present the beauty of the digital world. The machines are capable of performing a number of jobs with tiny electronic arms in split seconds and with accuracy.

The honest and loyal hacker steals and hides information for the benefit of the organization and is a boon to it, serving as a security cover and a force multiplier.

The unethical and dishonest hackers trade information for money and have the ability to make even the strong and mighty victims dance to their tunes.

Clever programming makes it possible to safeguard the interests of the nation and maintain secrecy. The honest hacker with strong programming skills is a potent shield and a weapon.

Both types of hackers are valued and patronized by the rulers to gain advantage over the adversary. The evil of a Digital Hacker is necessary to prevent the Earth from becoming Heaven.

CHAPTER 60

THE PEACEFUL ARMS DEALER

"Doll for the girl, the would be man handles guns
Gender traits stamped, before they learn to run;

A treat that's the living toy, life with toys a joy
A treat to evil gunman, a game with life they toy;

Mother's touch to cuddle up, Eves lay in the basket
Makers of ghostly Adams, for guns flocked to market;

Many a life saved if, toy-gun got parent's boot
Parents not pretend die, when sons' toy-guns shoot

To pretend bold one fathered, the gun–a masculine feature
Freezes a mother's warm heart, the cold metallic creature;

Children are made to play with toys with a gender bias from early childhood. The boy gets a gun whereas the girl plays with a doll.

Parents enjoy with the living toys–their children. Children are happy to play and learn with toys. The gunman enjoys the life threatening game played with others.

The girls play with mothers and other girls and are restricted in their movements. That makes them decent women. The boys are the masculine Adams for whom markets are flooded with guns and other fancy weapons.

Many people would be alive and not shot by gun trotting Adams, if parents had not played mock-dead when their son was shooting with toy-gun but had discouraged their son from playing with guns.

One invented the gun as a symbol of courage and masculinity. The same gun numbs a mother when the news of her loved ones killed in a shootout reaches her.

Hoped to borrow peace, to sleep in safety of lead

Life's final journey, the assassin's bullet led;

Guardian of life, the barrel, dictates a new lifestyle

Sanguine tears shed in barrels, cried the bereaved wife;

Seeds of fear beget gun fields, gains outweigh the loss

Barter gain with loss of life, sword seller and society cross;

Lifeless breathes out sulfur, life ceases to breathes

Life on lease lives, to place on lifeless, wreathe;

Schools confront forever, the insane bullet sprayer

Gun Grocer–a necessary evil, bear with solemn prayer."

People buy guns to feel safe and secure in the company of bullets. The very gun takes away their lives when a similar thinking person with a gun shoots them.

Possession of a gun has become a new fashion statement. Society encourages the trade by buying them instead of boycotting. A man loses blood in barrels and his hapless woman sheds tears in barrels.

Fear of losing life promotes the gun market. The profit that the business of gun gets far outweighs the loss. The seller and the society fight over the profit and loss of life.

The lifeless gun exhales fume of powder and the victim exhales life. Everyone's life is on lease, to place wreathes on the bodies of their departed loved ones.

School, the temple of learning, learns to live in constant fear of a trigger-happy lunatic. The evil of a Gun Grocer is necessary to prevent the Earth from becoming Heaven.

CHAPTER 61

THE HUMAN TRAFFIC REGULATORS

"Complex world of humans, filled with social oddities
Consumers end up consumed, as human commodities;

Nature deprived power, victim of fair-sex syndrome
Unfair to fair sex, males regulate freedom to roam;

Lucky to be born in races, that held in high esteem
Burden of propriety, honour for the Adam's team;

Lesser mortals the poor, labour born for slavery
Palace or a hut, served as dish so savoury;

In years of human bondage, women, children, young
No savior rebelled to free, frozen hands and tongue;

Human relations and demands are sometimes unnatural and strange. The society has become consumeristic in which even human beings are a commodity to be sold and bought.

Women, the fair sex, are considered weak as compared to men. Nature has reserved or gifted them with strength as per their role in the process of evolution. Yet, men decide the destiny of the women.

Women born in a society that respects them are lucky. They have to mind their ways as expected by men and then alone they are honourable members of the society.

The unlucky ones born to races that look down upon women as inferior beings are slaves to their men's diktats. However, in every society, women are treated as items of amusement.

The weak women folk, children and the vulnerable ones suffer for ages as there is no one to fight for their rights. There are only sermons and promises to offer.

Dread the elite full of life, to enter the lifeless world
Pity in heart's expanses, for crowded, crammed, curled;

Social visionaries watch, the exploited without remorse
Lash out hands and tongues, welfare schemes endorse;

Victim, victor caught in net, should savior plan a raid
Gives a slip the real beast, the one that propels the trade;

Should end to Eve's woes, expect from women in power
Many Eves bask in glory, on cursed nay fortunes shower;

Cast, baked, broken in hellfire, like fragile earthenware
Human trafficker–a necessary evil, bear with solemn prayer."

The powerful and the wealthy people avoid getting exposed to the inhuman treatment meted to the exploited ones. They feel pity for their condition but do nothing to improve them.

The social activists are numerous to put up a facade of benevolence. They blame the social apathy and the government's lack of will to help the victims. They plan grand projects for the welfare of the victims but do not act upon them.

When action is taken to catch the culprits, the victim and the trader are caught. The cunning trader escapes offering bribes, leaving the victim to suffer.

In a man's world if the women suffer, men can be blamed. Even in the rule of a woman in power, the situation does not improve. Some women enjoy power but do nothing for women, children and the vulnerable youth who continue to suffer.

Women, children, and the youth are treated as earthenware that can be molded, cast, and baked again and again. The evil of a Human Trafficker is necessary to prevent the Earth from becoming Heaven.

CHAPTER 62

THE UNREAL REALTOR

"Own a small piece of land, feel we own the Earth

Salutes the society, blessings bestowed, no dearth;

Gifted for free lifesaving puff, air for survival provided

Owner looks down from space, five elements divided;

Wander in social wilderness, some denied bit of land

Slither in dens illegal, residents of palaces grand;

Priceless deals struck unheard, penniless misery roars

Cloud of hope skips heaven's child, in estates richness pours;

Plots to snatch a plot to own, beams the proud landlord

At peace in block of dust, lives with neighbour in discord;

The owner of a small piece of land on this planet feels proud and secured as if one owns the whole Earth. The society also respects and salutes the owner addressing them as land lords.

The air that one breathes for dear life is given free by nature. The creator of the universe sees the creation being divided into elements, to be owned by the lowly human beings.

Some unlucky ones wander in search of a small piece of land to live but are denied one on this large planet. The lucky ones are gifted large chunks of land liberally, but illegally, and they build big palaces to live a luxurious life.

Shady land deals are carried out where the poor and miserable ones cry foul. Showers of welfare never wet the people living in the open. The shower fills the pale of the wealthy and the mighty ones.

One that deals in land, owns enough, but is ever ready to encroach upon other's land. The owner of a house sleeps peacefully only after disturbing the peace of the neighbour.

Crashed the gates with pulp, all those lived displaced

Forged a false ownership, legal heir's found misplaced;

For land, lands up in trouble, seen brothers at arms

None to hate this love, the love for land that harms;

A life's earning at stake, dear life hangs in balance

Paper legal frets and fumes, owners watch in silence;

Earth under the feet rattles, afraid to lose precious plot

Rightful owners lose the battle, under builder's onslaught;

Witness to the battle of land losers, on end stand the hair

Land Grabber–a necessary evil, bear with solemn prayer."

Fraudsters create fake documents to establish false ownership and forcibly vacate the true owners. The poor owners do not understand how the documents lied and they lost the ownership of their land.

Brothers come to blows over a piece of land and find themselves in trouble. There is hardly anyone who detests this love for land, though it causes so much of harm to the society.

People work hard and earn to make a home, to live peacefully. The cunning ones encroach upon their land and refuse to vacate. The legal battle threatens the very existence of the owner who had put all the life's earnings into it. Even with legal documents, one is made to wait for Law to declare the owner.

One's whole being is shaken on hearing the verdict. The rightful owner loses the land as the clever builders and the land mafia bribe their way to success.

The sordid tale of battle between the loser and the lawless gobblers of land terrifies the honest. The evil of a Land Grabber is necessary to prevent the Earth from becoming Heaven.

CHAPTER 63

THE DEFENDING CHAMPIONS

"Sustenance of life, nature ensures with show of strength

Deters not the violent humans, peaceful preaching at length;

From cradles to continents, life faces territorial tussle

Savage life forms fight, the civilized humans a puzzle

Heady minds for supremacy, see mighty crowns tumble

In streams runs blood sanguine, on roads tanks rumble;

Riding on ambition, to expand rule armies marched

Tortured and torched the defenders, left meadows parched;

Shrinks for new field to expand, killing machines perfected

Distant states fell to raiders, when mighty minds infected;

Survival of the organism in this world is governed by its ability to overcome hostile environment and prove its strength and will to live. Human beings with their intellect can overcome life threatening situations without a fight. Yet peaceful co-existence is not understood by them.

Everyone, from an infant to a nation, fights for space. Animals fight for territory and food supply, following the rules of nature. Human beings fighting for the same cause, though much civilized than the animals, defy reasoning.

The power-hungry fight for supremacy and the fight sees many mighty ones bite the dust. Where life giving water should flow, human blood flows and the road paved for human progress sees monster tanks spit fire.

Armies are commanded to march into enemy land, to kill, torture and capture them and their wealth. The green fields where grains grow are torched and destroyed.

When the human intellect is possessed by the evil of power, it creates weapons of mass destruction that can reach far and wide to conquer other's territory.

Designed to draw more blood, weapons execute with ease

Demand grows ever more, to doom self, pay hefty fees;

Suspicion the seed of war, states at war forever

Held gun over human faith, thrive death merchants clever;

Perched on stocks explosive, every nation to defend

Armed for mutual destruction, as saviors they pretend;

Silent sparks of conflict, turn into deafening war cry

Unseen warmongers, they rejoice when widows cry;

Proudly display martial pageantry, amidst haughty fanfare

War Monger—a necessary evil, bear with solemn prayer."

Weapons with more lethal power and capacity to draw more blood with less effort are invented and sold to ambitious heads. Demand for weapons for self-destruction grows as more and more nations feel insecure in the hostile environs.

Lack of faith in one another forces nations to prepare for war at all times. They prefer arms to faith for their safety. This suspicion benefits the ones who trade in weapons.

Nations stock up huge amount of weapons and ammunition to defend themselves. They pretend to save their people, but in reality, they are preparing to destroy one another.

Quarrels escalate into a war in no time. Blame the roar of the metallic beasts, human cries are not heard. The ones starting the war silently watch the battle and feel happy on counting the number of war widows on the other side of the fence.

The display of valour and chivalry in the glittering military ceremonies on victory over the enemy puts humanity to shame. The evil of a War Monger is necessary to prevent the Earth from becoming Heaven.

CHAPTER 64

THE PRINCIPLE TRADERS

"Have excess of gray matter, give air to own grudges

Blissful ignorance of own follies, mark of social judges;

Patrons of ethics old and ancient, arrived the moral police

Dispense values borrowed, grant principles on lease;

Rooted in self-deception, decide the right or wrong

Honouring self-perception, reserve the right to wrong;

Treasure of ethnic traditions, prophets, self-styled preserve

Tune the masses to trust, decide what people deserve;

Hijack social issues to stay, they organize syndicate

Vow to cleanse maladies, crook and criminal vindicate;

There exists a class of people who display more wisdom than they really possess. They are ready to point fingers at others but are unaware of their own follies.

These self-styled custodians of ethics and morality assume the role of the moral police. They lend principles and morals to the society because they claim their propriety.

They believe themselves to be always right and decide what is wrong or right for the society. These self-righteous ones reserved the right to do wrong.

The custodians of ancient tradition and wisdom see themselves as Prophets, command trust and obedience from the masses and decide the treatment people deserve.

The moral police interfere in all social issues and debate over them in polarized groups. The practitioners of immorality defend themselves to set the social evils right.

With speeches verbose, they target the young brigade

Did ever question self or parents, with morals who trade;

For verbal stone-pelters million, struggle for life a non-issue

Moral values on the slide, on trivial issues lose a shoe;

Green horns build no appetite, for hefty funds to digest

Thousand limbs for social cause, make social work a jest;

Daggers drawn to stitch together, fabric torn asunder

Battle immoral on morals rages, masses to destiny surrender;

Regale in mental duels, to labour none to spare

Immoral Prophet–a necessary evil, bear with solemn prayer."

The youth are their prime target whom they want to reform with sermons on ethics and morality. They never challenge the wisdom of the older generation that actually governs the society.

The war of words is their main activity with scant regards for the daily grind of the masses. Social morality is on the wane but the battle for verbal supremacy goes on.

The young generation has no power over the grants and funds received for the welfare activities of the society. They do not usurp them. There are others, who volunteer for social work only to share the loot of funds.

Social workers and the moral police continue their struggle against the declining moral standards. The social evils multiply without respite for the poor masses.

The social warriors are busy in verbal duels over principles and have no time to spare for the cleansing of the society. The evil of an Immoral Prophet is necessary to prevent the Earth from becoming Heaven.

CHAPTER 65

THE WEALTHY BEGGARS

"Pedestal of greed and grandeur, the need of vice and noble

Cradle of vice and virtues, **Desire** the mother of all trouble;

Penniless attract more miseries, more attracts more riches

Carpet laid for rich shoppers, pauper rags of misfortune stitches;

With right to rob the rights, they gift disguised as charity

Heirs–apparent of benevolence, attempt parity with almighty;

The rich hawks issue threats, for dove money a threat

Feed on morsels starved thin, the claws if fail they fret;

One made peace with destiny, priceless bought at a price

Time knows no rich noble enough, who stands witness to despise;

Both, the evil and the noble people, have desires that invoke greed and hatred. They want to occupy the seat of power. This desire is the root cause of all misdeeds.

Wealth does not visit the home of the poor, miserable folks but follows the rich. The rich are showered with luxuries and the poor reel under poverty.

The rich rob the poor of their rightful share and oblige them by doing charity. They display benevolence and act as the saviors of the underprivileged.

The rich intimidate the poor by their might and wealth. The poor see the desire for money a threat to their life. The poor live on morsels spared by the rich but the rich ones get furious on losing an opportunity to make more money.

The poor and the weak are content with whatever comes their way and hope to live peacefully. They pay dearly, just to survive. No rich and powerful one is noble enough to oppose the exploitation of the poor.

Quiet flows the wealth, to build up for destruction huge

Pounce on each ounce of meat, siphon from drop to deluge;

Ambitions sky high of riches, from hut to palace transform

Imperial designs welcome, desire the society to reform;

Bow down to riches unseen, even sages fall from grace

Custodians of wealth ill earned, holy, vile rush to embrace;

Glitter and glare blind vision, with radiant wealth in excess

In the light of fortune's beacon, hides the unholy nexus;

Acts of defiance of power, or riches put to shame are rare

Raunchy Rich—a necessary evil, bear with solemn prayer."

The greed of the rich and the ambitious slowly but surely erodes the foundation of the society. They gobble the share of the people drop by drop and thus flood their chests with wealth.

Wealth thus accumulated transforms the small houses of the rich into huge palaces. They transform themselves into fat social borers and yet expect the society to progress.

The wealthy are so powerful that even the wise and holy ones bow before them. The power of money made by unfair means draws the wise and the vice into their folds.

The evil power of excess wealth blinds people. They ignore the misdeeds of the blessed accumulator of wealth and resign to their fate.

There are very few people who stand up to face the powerful and belittle them. The evil of the Raunchy Rich is necessary to prevent the Earth from becoming Heaven.

CHAPTER 66

THE JUDICIOUS PROSECUTOR

"All dread and shun the legal course, a maze of slimy laws

A bolt of misfortune welcome, not the lawyer's claws;

Set endless rules and dates, the battle turned to a sport

Pleaders play with justice, the criminals turn to court;

Missed the fortune's call, neither drank nor ate

Price paid for pleading, saw lawyer's infant graduate;

Met with professional assurances, legal door you knocked

Saw hope with time sublimate, felt timely justice mocked;

A test of nerves for the rights, filled naïve with rage

Flew crafty ones to freedom, gullible ones to cage;

People want justice for them but avoid the legal path. The legal procedures are full of incomprehensible laws for a common citizen. One would bear the inconvenience of injustice, rather than getting tortured by the legal proceedings.

The legal case offers only dates, rules and summons, and turns the legal fight into a sport for the legal professionals. The stakeholders mock the system and hence only the unfair ones turn to court as they are hopeful of delaying justice to the honest ones.

The honest ones trapped in a legal battle curse their fortune and lose sleep and meals due to fear of losing the battle. They keep funding the lawyers who thrive on the victim's misery.

Every lawyer one approaches, assures of justice to the client. As time passes the client loses hope in the legal system and becomes a mere witness to the mocking game.

Legal cases are a tough test of one's patience. The hopeful ones lose their cool often, because they find the culprits escaping unharmed and the poor seeker of justice getting punished.

Drama sordid enough, for a sage to turn violent

The false cried the loudest, justice kept silent;

Traveled the path to realize, legal the last resort

They prod the weary traveler, the last penny to extort;

Patrons of quick justice, seldom deliver a judgment lawful

Lives through the nightmare awake, to narrate a saga awful;

Wears a million masks, that hide the real face

Frees the mocking outlaws, on goes the eternal race;

Twist the laws elastic, with money from circle to square

Listless Lawyer–a necessary evil, bear with solemn prayer."

The legal battles turn so unfair that even the most balanced and patient hermit would be enraged by the injustice meted to the honest. Those who commit crime are the noisiest ones before whom even the lawyers observe silence.

The victims repent for the decision to approach the court for justice after the horrific experiences. The lawyers relentlessly persuade them to carry on the battle to extract as much money as they can.

The judicial system promises the citizens quick deliverance of justice. The outcome is neither in time nor is just. The loser lives the dreadful dream with eyes open to tell the story of a judicial nightmare.

Law has many forms and figures to hide the truth and not let the real nature to be revealed. Chained in dishonesty, it frees the criminals and lives up to its nature.

Money and power change the decisions in their favour as laws are tailored to be tampered with. The evil of a Dishonest Lawyer is necessary to prevent the Earth from becoming Heaven.

CHAPTER 67

THE DIVINE GROCER

"Permeates national borders, to form parties global

Principles supreme to preach, words and deeds ignoble;

Swooned with divine lullaby, the holy sedatives clever

Crowds swayed in frenzy, spiritual stupor lasts forever;

Promises savage salvation, with subtle messages concealed

For young initiate in spiritual folds, escape routes sealed;

Burden believers with blasphemy, all outfits the same

Mischief not one's nature, other faiths to blame;

Estranged from relations, relate with near and far

Believers stuffed with hatred, prepare for holy war;

Party of believers are formed transcending the national borders and infiltrating the territories of the non-believers. Lofty ideas and ideals are floated to trap the ignorant and to exploit them, once victimized.

The innocent and the ignorant are carried away by the sweet talks of the holy ones. Once addicted to a particular faith and inducted into a party, the crowd dances to the holy tunes losing the faculty of discrimination.

The spiritual facade cleverly hides enslavement and promises boons of liberation and salvation to the followers. Once trapped in a holy trap, one finds it difficult to escape.

When one tries to revolt and break free, one is declared a heretic and cursed. All faiths claim to be above others and blame one another for the degradation of the spiritual values in the world.

The believers are divided and pulled away from their relations and friends due to their belief. They try to relate and get close to believers living far away. They are so averse to the ideas and beliefs of other sects and religions that they can contemplate on waging a war.

Promise all mighty to bind, minds cohesive that believe

Almighty shies away from skeptic, if differ in thought, leave;

Cast spell on the gullible, believers they en-masse dupe

Shun heretic that suspects, welcome the likeminded group;

Submissive faith one displays, the blind receives blessings

Ushered to doorsteps of Heaven, one to their tune sings;

United to divide the world, glad to criticize are all

Lead you away from The Almighty, on their feet you fall;

Glorifying self to mute others, deafening speakers blare

Rogue Divinity–a necessary evil, bear with solemn prayer."

All the mighty and spiritually powerful promise the believers to bond them with The Almighty. The Almighty disowns those who do not confirm and are banished from the syndicate.

The simple and naive ones are spellbound witnessing the grand spiritual facade. They are served well and their woes are attended to. The non-believers are distanced and expelled.

One who follows the holy syndicate without questioning receives blessings from the holy ones. Surrender to the spiritual will begets an entry to Heaven.

Every sect, every religion unites people to divide the world into believers and non-believers and criticizes another's faith. People worship those who actually lead the faithful away from their creator.

They resort to noisy propaganda and advertise their religion and beliefs to silence the competitors. The evil of a Divine Rogue is necessary to prevent the Earth from becoming Heaven.

CHAPTER 68

THE ADMINIS-TRAITOR

"From wilderness to heaven, built stairs to corridors of power
Ruler-lord's cloud-maker, on whom the fortunes shower;

Planned to miss good deeds, misdeeds but glorified
Lied in peace the traitors, against truth a hundred lied;

Piled facts and figures, to ascend wisdom's throne
Heart that beat when served, unserved turned to stone;

Honour self with perks, plead all hands to unite
Demand a penny more, with clenched fists they fight;

Symbol of civic synergy, the stately servants' troop
To grab a share of loot, how much low they stoop;

The young citizens who aspire to govern the nation, work hard to reach the corridors of power. They assist the leaders to rule and are liberally honoured.

Actions and plans meant for the benefit of the people are ignored. The projects beneficial to them and their political masters are glorified. Those who were supposed to expose untruth, kept silent, but spoke strongly against the truth.

They play with cooked up facts and statistics and display their wisdom. The heart of wisdom worked and obliged till served but lost all interest to serve the people once not obliged.

They pay themselves lavishly and are all united in claiming hefty perks. When the rightful unite to demand their share, they fight them with all their might.

The mighty clan of the loyal servants of the state displays rare unity to fight for their share of the nation's loot. The best brains of the nation fall from grace to fill their wallet.

A colluding force to tame, a corrosive force to wield

Unyielding servants rule, the mighty rulers yield;

Ambitious lot on wings, raise the stakes sky high

Fields of bribe fertile, fiscal rivers run dry;

One in million a success, young minds ignited

Elderly wisdom put out, the stars in politics slighted;

Trust reposed in wisdom, few think to pay back

For illegal approvals, busy counting the pay-back

Jewels overpriced, with borrowed glitter and glare

Uncivilized Servant–a necessary evil, bear with solemn prayer."

When the stately servants unite to fight against those who care not for their interests, they are a force to reckon with. Even the leaders yield to their unfair demands.

The vastly read and educated servants are highly ambitious and take corruption to astronomical proportions. The quantum of financial misappropriation empties the state coffers.

Millions of young students aspire to be in the saddle of governance but a very few are selected. These bright and learned young citizens of the nation leave their moral wisdom and try to outsmart their political masters in practicing worldly wisdom.

People trust these educated, bright young lot of administrators and expect them to bring a change in the ways of governance. Most of them forget their duty and are busy making a fortune for themselves.

They are the ones whose fleeting value and worth as good administrators is exaggerated and is blown out of proportion. The evil of an Uncivilized Servant is necessary to prevent the Earth from becoming Heaven.

CHAPTER 69

THE SOVEREIGN LEADER

"They stage-set the scenes, the servants' mind perceived

Leaders of the Servants lord over, an idea servant conceived;

Seeking hands humble lips, the epitome of humility

Crown of power bites the dust, to gain credibility;

Thief over a robber elect, the beggars have a choice

Hapless voter elects them, and in their victory rejoice;

Heed not for the past deeds, leader's win you celebrate

Lose not chance to profit, on whose loss do deliberate;

Money and muscle the yardstick, for leader to qualify

Clean one not yet fit to lead, the character first vilified;

The political servants voted to power by the people design the structure of government. They are the servants but control and dictate the people who voted them to power.

Before the elections, the leaders humbly beg the voters to elect them. Their arrogance and pride vanishes when they seek votes with folded hands.

The begging leaders choose a less corrupt candidate over a bigger crook in the opposition party to convince the people. The voter is left with no choice but to elect the lesser crook, nevertheless, a crook.

The voters celebrate the victory of their leader on winning the election, forgetting the past wrong doings. People look for their profit without thinking about the loot of the nation's wealth by the very leader.

The society listens to one who torment them with their criminal gangs and the power of money. The honest and fair player would lose the election as the voters find such a candidate unfit to rule.

Ruler, Ruled, both accused, each one cries foul play

Trusting time, the election time, solidarity they display;

Favour's flavour lingers on, you hardly smell a rat

Victor tastes sweet revenge, calls it tit for tat;

Dwarfs jump in battle royal, when mindless giants clash

Where verbal duels leaders play, lowly beings mash;

Masses and leaders in fray, cry Politics when wronged

To embrace stooges in Politics, a million masses thronged;

Enthroned in people's mind, good governance slayer

Polemic Politician–a necessary evil, bear with solemn prayer."

The leader and also the people, are to be blamed for the maladies of the society. When election approaches, they forget their differences and display unity that is born out of selfishness.

The leaders bribe the voters and promise them illegitimate favours without raising any suspicion. Victory is settling of old scores by the winning candidate of the ruling party. The vengeful game goes on.

The lowly voters and party workers show much enthusiasm in the elections where their mighty leaders fight. The leaders are engaged in harmless arguments whereas the workers engage in brawls and risk their lives for the victory of their leader.

Those who are adept in the art of governance and elections, accuse the opposition of playing Politics when they taste defeat or are caught resorting to unfair means. Yet the masses fight for their victory and worship them as gods.

The political leaders find a place of reverence in the minds and souls of their followers though they trample upon their very lives. The evil of a Politician, ever in dispute and controversies, is necessary to prevent the Earth from becoming Heaven.

CHAPTER 70

THE SHOW MUST GO ON

Said the Devoted:

"Politics, the mill of governance, turned in all ages
Grinding servants, masters, kings, and divine sages;

Hands that beg for votes to serve, know profits are great
Each one sure of share of loot, though a little late;

Tragic mill of governance turns, till subjects lie
Magical ways of politics, where servant's rules apply;

Dis-service to unjust kings, sees just provider doomed
Indifference and mass differences, let consumers consumed;

Prey fuels the volcano, dormant sits the predator
Servant prods the subjects, to roll into the crater;

The Devoted said:

Politics has been preached and practiced since ages. It has influenced and touched the lives of all types of people and personalities in all sections of the societies around the world.

Those who seek votes with folded hands like beggars, do so knowing well that the end result will be worth the humiliation. They will taste success sooner or later, but the long wait is worth the rewards.

The deplorable state of politics where people are exploited and deprived will continue till the people are selfish and insincere in electing their leaders. The ones who are elected to serve the people will lord over them. Such is the strange matrix of politics.

Neglect of the political gods brings misery to the voters. Differences between various factions of the society and political parties, coupled with the careless attitude of the people toward Political Awareness & Education makes them ideal prey for the political predators.

Voters are the prime factor in the process of election and politics. The leaders wait for them to submit themselves to their leader's service. They then push the followers into the electoral battlefield.

In a rare show of honesty, the predator becomes the prey

Never ever the voter, loser curses the unfortunate day;

You cast your pricey vote, and expect me to operate

Both equal partners in service, would you not cooperate;

Should your clan not stake, self-respect to please

Would meet leaders honest, who know not to fleece;

If my clan steers, away from the battlefield

Would lose all power, and fight without a shield;

Beware of pitfalls, let bygone be bygone

Says Devoted to Devotee, **"The show must go on."**

The one who wants to win, plays victim to gain sympathy, displaying rare honesty and thanks the voters for the victory. The loser never blames the voters but the winner or one's stars for the loss.

The voters cast their vote and think their duty is over. They leave the governance to the leader and expect to be served by hook or even by crook. Both, the leader and the voter, should work together and have equal responsibilities in running the show.

If the voters do not compromise honesty for their personal benefits and stoop down to please their leader for petty favours, they would elect honest and responsible leaders.

If the leaders are disillusioned or discouraged by the murky state of politics and step back, they will be out of the race for power and position. That would leave them vulnerable to the opponent's attack.

Get educated on the nuances of politics, taking lessons from the past to avoid misery in future and march forward to continue striving for a better governance. Says the Devoted, "The eternal game of politics must be carried forward for a better future."